CHRISTIAN MORALS

Cambridge University Press
Fetter Lane, London

New York, Bombay, Calcutta
Madras, Toronto
Macmillan

Tokyo
Maruzen-Kabushiki-Kaisha

SIR THOMAS BROWNE'S
CHRISTIAN MORALS

THE SECOND EDITION
WITH THE *LIFE* OF THE AUTHOR

BY

SAMUEL JOHNSON, LL.D.

Edited
With an Introduction and Notes
by
S. C. ROBERTS

CAMBRIDGE
At the UNIVERSITY PRESS
1927

KRAUS REPRINT CO.
New York
1969

*My grateful thanks are due to Mr E.
Harrison for his help in proof-reading and
in the identification of several allusions.
I am also indebted to Dr M. R. James,
Dr A. B. Cook, Mr L. F. Powell and
Mr A. Attwater for similar help.*

S. C. R.

First published 1927
Reprinted by permission of the Cambridge University Press
KRAUS REPRINT CO.
A U.S. Division of Kraus-Thomson Organization Limited

Printed in U.S.A.

CONTENTS

INTRODUCTION

§ 1. *Christian Morals*

THOUGH many times reprinted in conjunction with other works, *Christian Morals* has not often been separately published. It was one of the last works Sir Thomas Browne wrote before his death in 1682 and the manuscript, after having been mislaid either by Dr Edward Browne or by Archbishop Tenison, was first printed at Cambridge in 1716. The editor was John Jeffery, Archdeacon of Norwich, who published the work "from the Original and Correct Manuscript of the Author," this manuscript embodying the concluding paragraphs of *A Letter to a Friend* (1690).

The second edition, with notes and a *Life* of Browne by Dr Johnson, was published in 1756 and the third edition (a re-issue of the second with a new title-page) in 1761; separate reprints were also published in 1863 and 1904. Johnson's notes were reprinted and supplemented by Wilkin in his edition of the *Works* (1835–6), and Greenhill added copious notes in his edition of *Religio Medici, A Letter to a Friend &c. and Christian Morals* (1881). Nevertheless, the byways of Browne's, as well as of Johnson's, learning still afford material for additional commentary.[1]

Posthumously published and lacking the author's final revision, *Christian Morals* is commonly reckoned as one of the lesser lights in the firmament of Sir Thomas Browne's prose.

"Has Mr Johnson sent you his new edition of Sir Thomas Browne's Christian Morals?" wrote Miss Talbot to Mrs Carter; "'Tis a collection of the noblest thoughts, drest in the uncouthest language possible, for which reason few will read, and half of those despise, a book as superior to Mr Greville's[2] as Epictetus to Tom Thumb."

The work has, indeed, been likened to "an elaborate and magnificent parody of the Book of Proverbs," but it is highly characteristic of Browne that he should have infused into a

[1] Greenhill points out that the notes to the 1756 edition are not specifically ascribed to Johnson. But the stylistic evidence of such a note as that on p. 132 of this edition is surely convincing.

[2] Fulke Greville, *Maxims, characters, and reflections . . .* (1756).

gnomic essay that same combination of grandeur and *bizarrerie* which is found in his better known works. However trite the text, or however brief the homily, Browne's learning, like the cheerfulness of the immortal Mr Edwards, "will keep breaking in." To illustrate a paragraph on self-control, Browne invokes a pageant in which Lapithytes and Centaurs, Caesar and Alexander, Cato and Origen are brought clearly before the reader's vision; Plautus and Cicero, Sidonius and Machiavelli are quoted to emphasise a warning against severity towards small mistakes. Sometimes Browne opens his exhortation with a certain simplicity:

Let the characters of good things stand indelibly in thy mind and thy thoughts be active on them.

But the web of imagery is quickly woven:

To thoughtful observators, the whole world is a phylactery.... Happy are they who verify their amulets, and make their phylacteries speak in their lives and actions.... When death's-heads on our hands have no influence upon our heads, and fleshless cadavers abate not the exorbitances of the flesh; when crucifixes upon mens' hearts suppress not their bad commotions, and his image who was murdered for us withholds not from blood and murder; phylacteries prove but formalities, and their despised hints sharpen our condemnations.

Or again, Browne's descant upon the plainsong of hypocrisy is characteristic:

Behold thyself by inward opticks and the crystalline of thy soul.... The greatest imperfection is in our inward sight, that is, to be ghosts unto our own eyes....

There is little of "novity" in the fundaments of Browne's ethics. He is concerned primarily to be "a moralist of the mount," but he does not set too low a value upon what was for him a "courtly and splendid world." Browne, who exhorted men to "sit quiet in the soft showers of PROVIDENCE," had no cause, as Johnson had, to describe his own life as "radically wretched," nor did he share Johnson's "secret horrour of the last." He contemplated death without fear and the next world with a kind of Christian ἀταραξία:

All which [i.e. earthly inequalities] may be contentedly allowable in the affairs and ends of this world, and in suspension unto what will be in the order of things hereafter, and the new system of mankind which will be in the world to come; when the last may be the first, and the first the last; when Lazarus may sit above Caesar, and the just obscure on earth shall shine like the sun in heaven; when personations shall cease, and histrionism of happiness be over; when reality shall rule, and all shall be as they shall be for ever.

§ 2. *Browne and Johnson*

For some years after the publication of the *Dictionary* in 1755 Johnson was still writing for bread; the fame of his *magnum opus* "had not set him above the necessity of making provision for the day that was passing over him." It was in the early months of 1756 that he was saved from a debtor's prison by Samuel Richardson, and the "little book" which he sent to his friend in token of gratitude for his deliverance may very well have been the second edition of *Christian Morals*. If further evidence be sought for Johnson's continued dependence upon his pen, it is but necessary to recall his contributions, in the year 1756, to Kit Smart's *Universal Visiter*, his reviews for the *Literary Magazine*, his prefaces to Rolt's

Dictionary of Trade and Payne's *Game of Draughts*, and the "preliminary discourse" for the first number of *The London Chronicle*.

In one sense, then, the edition of *Christian Morals* must be considered as part of Johnson's regular work in Grub Street. On the other hand, it was a task to which he must have turned *con amore*.

The particular flavour of Browne's scholarship was highly agreeable to Johnson's taste. It is true that in the sale-catalogue of his library only one of Browne's works is to be found, but that one is *Vulgar Errors* and the *Dictionary* abounds in quotations from it. Johnson's thirst for out-of-the-way knowledge was insatiable, and though *The Anatomy of Melancholy* can alone claim the supreme distinction of making Johnson an early riser, it may be safely conjectured that the fascination of *Vulgar Errors* was only one degree less powerful.

Further, Browne's profession struck a sympathetic chord in one whose interest in medicine was both practical and academic. Himself an amateur physician and an enthusiastic dabbler in chemistry, Johnson took more than a friendly interest in the maladies of his friends and contributed a preface, and possibly some articles, to the *Medicinal Dictionary* of Dr James. The intimate friend of Bathurst and many other physicians, he wrote short lives of Boerhaave and Sydenham and his own library contained many medical works, from the *editio princeps* of Aretaeus, *De Causis Morborum* to Cheselden's *Anatomy* and Cheyne's *English Malady*.

But Browne was more than a scholarly physician; he was a man of science who assumed "the honourable Stile of a Christian." We know little of the early period of Johnson's life in which he became "a sort of lax talker against religion," but he always commented with satisfaction upon any man of learning, who, after a period of infidelity, recovered his belief in Christianity, especially if such belief should be "salvifically" tinged; the fact that Browne was not only a Christian but a Christian moralist was a further recommendation to the author of *The Rambler*, and if a bond of sentiment be also sought, it may be found in Pembroke College, Oxford.

Yet the relationship between Browne and Johnson which is most commonly cited has not yet been mentioned—the alleged similarity of literary style. "Sir Thomas Browne," writes Boswell, "whose life Johnson wrote was fond of Anglo-Latian diction; and to his example we are to ascribe Johnson's sometimes indulging himself in this kind of phraseology," and in a note he adds: "The observation of his having imitated Sir Thomas Brown has been made by many people; and lately it has been insisted on, and illustrated by a variety of quotations from Brown, in one of the popular Essays written by the Reverend Mr Knox."

The Reverend Mr Vicesimus Knox is not wholly convincing. He expresses the common view that Browne "preferred polysyllabic expressions derived from the language of ancient Rome, to his vernacular vocabulary" and quotes a few phrases from *Vulgar Errors*, such as "reminiscential evocation," "constant manuduction," "deuteroscopy" and others, to prove that they were the model on which the style of *The Rambler* was constructed.[1] Nor is the sentence selected by Robertson from Johnson's *Frederick the*

[1] *Winter Evenings, or Lucubrations on Life and Letters*, XII

Great such a glaring example of "Anglo-Latian diction" as to provoke extravagant comment:

To review this *towering* regiment was his daily pleasure; and to perpetuate it was so much his care that when he met a tall woman he immediately commanded one of his *Titanian* retinue to marry her, that they might *propagate procerity.*

That Johnson shared Browne's fondness for Latin derivatives is not to be denied, but Murphy was probably right when he observed that:

in the course of that work [the *Dictionary*] as he grew familiar with technical and scholastic words, he thought that the bulk of his readers were equally learned; or at least would admire the splendour and dignity of the style.

The Rambler has always offered tempting material to the imitator, but the cruder sort of Johnsonian parodist is liable to bring more ridicule upon himself than upon Johnson. When, for instance, the author of *Lexiphanes* wrote: "I bibulated the salubrity of our most amiable sovereign, the safe parturition of his transcendental consort, and the happy encrease of the sons and daughters of Britannick royalty," his parody ceased to have any critical value. As Johnson himself said, "The imitators of my style have not hit it" and though Latin forms came most naturally to him, it is noteworthy that when he revised his work, the revision was always in the direction of simplicity.[1]

That Johnson recognised the dangers of "a mixture of heterogeneous words brought together from distant regions" is clear from the well-known passage in his *Life* of Browne,[2] and in the *Dictionary* there is more than one example of the condemnation of a word used by Browne as exotic or unnecessary.[3] Moreover, Johnson's annotation of *Christian Morals* throws an interesting light on the development of the English language; he found it necessary to explain *precocity* and *stenography*, but not *extances* or *exantlation*.

Browne and Johnson have also challenged comparison as masters of "the other harmony of prose." From the point of view of rhythmical technique, it has been maintained

[1] See Nichol Smith in *C.H.E.L.* x, 187.
[2] p. 49.
[3] See notes on pp. 126 and 171.

xvi

that "a characteristic sentence of Johnson and a characteristic sentence of Sir Thomas could only be compared, as regards rhythm, by an ear so dull as to be *ab initio* disqualified,"[1] and even to the layman it is clear that while the symmetry of Johnson's prose architecture is the product of disciplined scholarship combined with an ear for linguistic cadence, the rhythmical triumphs of Sir Thomas Browne are the work of genius.

Johnson wrote for a living. Had he followed his personal inclination, he might have preferred to compile a work on the Curiosities of the English Language rather than a Dictionary. But the booksellers pressed him for a Dictionary and Johnson wrote little except under the pressure of poverty and of the booksellers. Long years in Grub Street made him a little contemptuous of those authors for whom the writing of books was a graceful hobby or an academic pastime. "The reciprocal civility of authors," he wrote, "is one of the most risible scenes in the farce of life," and he comments with rather a heavy literalness upon Browne's descrip-

[1] Saintsbury, *English Prose Rhythm*, p. 267.

tion of his own life as a miracle of thirty years:

A scholastick and academical life is very uniform; and has, indeed, more safety than pleasure. A traveller has greater opportunities of adventure; but Browne traversed no unknown seas or Arabian desarts; and, surely, a man may visit France and Italy, reside at Montpellier and Padua, and at last take his degree at Leyden without any thing miraculous.

Similarly Browne's contention that "mankind is comprehended in a few faces"[1] is too much for Johnson. The whole section, he says, is "very fanciful and indefensible." Here, perhaps, there may be a hint of some fundamental difference between the seventeenth and eighteenth centuries—between the century which experimented and the century which found itself.

Nevertheless, the temperamental bond between Browne and Johnson was a strong one. Browne's memory, said Whitefoot, was "capacious and tenacious, insomuch as he remembred all that was remarkable in any book that he had read.... In the Latin poets he remembred every thing that was acute and

[1] pp. 127 ff.

pungent; he had read most of the historians, antient and modern, wherein his observations were singular, not taken notice of by common readers; he was excellent company when he was at leisure...."

Here, indeed, was a man after Johnson's own heart, a man, who, in Johnson's words, will not easily be deprived of the esteem of posterity, "while learning shall have any reverence among men."

THE LIFE

OF

SIR THOMAS BROWNE
Kt., M.D.

BY

Samuel Johnson
LL.D.

THE LIFE OF
SIR THOMAS BROWNE

THOUGH the writer of the following ESSAYS feems to have had the fortune common among men of letters, of raifing little curiofity after his private life, and has, therefore, few memorials preferved of his felicities or misfortunes; yet, becaufe an edition of a pofthumous work appears imperfect and neglected, without fome account of the author, it was thought neceffary to attempt the gratification of that curiofity which naturally inquires, by what peculiarities of nature or fortune eminent men have been diftinguished, how uncommon attainments have been gained, and what influence learning has had on its poffeffors, or virtue on its teachers.

SIR THOMAS BROWNE was born at London, in the parish of St. Michael in Cheapfide, on the 19th of October, MDCV. [a] His father was a merchant of an antient family at Upton in Cheshire. Of the name or family of his mother, I find no account.

[a] Life of Sir THOMAS BROWNE, prefixed to the antiquities of Norwich.

OF his childhood or youth, there is little known; except that he loft his father very early; that he was, according to the common [a] fate of orphans, defrauded by one of his guardians; and that he was placed for his education at the fchool of Winchefter.

His mother, having taken [b] three thoufand pounds, as the third part of her husband's property, left her fon, by confequence, fix thoufand; a large fortune for a man deftined to learning, at that time when commerce had not yet filled the nation with nominal riches. But it happened to him as to many others, to be made poorer by opulence; for his mother soon married Sir THOMAS DUTTON, probably by the inducement of her fortune; and he was left to the rapacity of his guardian, deprived now of both his parents, and therefore helplefs and unprotected.

HE was removed in the beginning of the year MDCXXIII from Winchefter to Oxford; [c] and entered a gentleman-commoner of Broadgate-Hall, which was foon afterwards

[a] Whitefoot's character of Sir THOMAS BROWNE in a marginal note.
[b] Life of Sir THOMAS BROWNE.
[c] Wood's Athenæ Oxonienfes.

endowed, and took the name of Pembroke-College, from the EARL OF PEMBROKE then chancellor of the Univerfity. He was admitted to the degree of bachelor of arts, January 31, MDCXXVI-VII; being, as WOOD remarks, the firft man of eminence graduated from the new college, to which the zeal or gratitude of thofe that love it moft, can wish little better, than that it may long proceed as it began.

HAVING afterwards taken his degree of mafter of arts, he turned his ftudies to phyfick, [a] and practifed it for fome time in Oxfordshire; but foon afterwards, either induced by curiofity, or invited by promifes, he quitted his fettlement, and accompanied his [b] father-in-law, who had fome employment in Ireland, in a vifitation of the forts and caftles, which the ftate of Ireland then made neceffary.

HE that has once prevailed on himfelf to break his connexions of acquaintance, and begin a wandering life, very eafily continues it. Ireland had, at that time, very little to offer to the obfervation of a man of letters: he, therefore, paffed [c] into France and Italy;

[a] WOOD.
[b] Life of Sir THOMAS BROWNE.   [c] Ibid.

made fome ftay at Montpellier and Padua, which were then the celebrated fchools of phyfick; and returning home through Holland, procured himfelf to be created Doctor of phyfick at Leyden.

WHEN he began his travels, or when he concluded them, there is no certain account; nor do there remain any obfervations made by him in his paffage through thofe countries which he vifited. To confider, therefore, what pleafure or inftruction might have been received from the remarks of a man fo curious and diligent, would be voluntarily to indulge a painful reflection, and load the imagination with a wish, which, while it is formed, is known to be vain. It is, however, to be lamented, that thofe who are moft capable of improving mankind, very frequently neglect to communicate their knowledge; either becaufe it is more pleafing to gather ideas than to impart them, or becaufe to minds naturally great, few things appear of fo much importance as to deferve the notice of the publick.

ABOUT the year MDCXXXIV, [a] he is fuppofed to have returned to London; and the

[a] Biographia Britannica.

next year to have written his celebrated treatife, called RELIGIO MEDICI, "The Religion of a Phyfician," [a] which he declares himfelf never to have intended for the prefs, having compofed it only for his own exercife and entertainment. It, indeed, contains many paffages, which, relating merely to his own perfon, can be of no great importance to the publick: but when it was written, it happened to him as to others, he was too much pleafed with his performance, not to think that it might pleafe others as much; he, therefore, communicated it to his friends, and receiving, I fuppofe, that exuberant applaufe with which every man repays the grant of perufing a manufcript, he was not very diligent to obftruct his own praife by recalling his papers, but fuffered them to wander from hand to hand, till at laft, without his own confent, they were in MDCXLII given to a printer.

THIS has, perhaps, fometimes befallen others; and this, I am willing to believe, did really happen to Dr. BROWNE: but there is, furely, fome reafon to doubt the truth of the

[a] Letter to Sir KENELM DIGBY, prefixed to the Religio Medici, folio edit.

complaint fo frequently made of furreptitious editions. A fong, or an epigram, may be eafily printed without the author's knowledge; becaufe it may be learned when it is repeated, or may be written out with very little trouble: but a long treatife, however elegant, is not often copied by mere zeal or curiofity, but may be worn out in paffing from hand to hand, before it is multiplied by a tranfcript. It is eafy to convey an imperfect book, by a diftant hand, to the prefs, and plead the circulation of a falfe copy as an excufe for publishing the true, or to correct what is found faulty or offenfive, and charge the errors on the tranfcriber's depravations.

THIS is a ftratagem, by which an author panting for fame, and yet afraid of feeming to challenge it, may at once gratify his vanity, and preferve the appearance of modefty; may enter the lifts, and fecure a retreat: and this, candour might fuffer to pafs undetected as an innocent fraud, but that indeed no fraud is innocent; for the confidence which makes the happinefs of fociety, is in fome degree diminished by every man, whofe practice is at variance with his words.

THE RELIGIO MEDICI was no fooner

published than it excited the attention of the publick, by the novelty of paradoxes, the dignity of fentiment, the quick fucceffion of images, the multitude of abftrufe allufions, the fubtlety of difquifition, and the ftrength of language.

WHAT is much read, will be much criticifed. The EARL OF DORSET recommended this book to the perufal of Sir KENELM DIGBY, who returned his judgment upon it, not in a letter, but a book; in which, though mingled with fome pofitions fabulous and uncertain, there are acute remarks, juft cenfures, and profound fpeculations, yet its principal claim to admiration is, that ᵃ it was written in twenty-four hours, of which part was fpent in procuring BROWNE's book, and part in reading it.

OF thefe animadverfions, when they were yet not all printed, either officioufnefs or malice informed Dr. BROWNE; who wrote to Sir KENELM with much foftnefs and cere-mony, declaring the unworthinefs of his work to engage fuch notice, the intended privacy of the compofition, and the corruptions of the

ᵃ DIGBY's letter to BROWNE, prefixed to the Religio Medici, folio edit.

impreffion; and received an anfwer equally
gentle and refpectful, containing high com-
mendations of the piece, pompous profeffions
of reverence, meek acknowledgments of inability, and anxious apologies for the haftinefs
of his remarks.

THE reciprocal civility of authors is one of
the moft rifible fcenes in the farce of life. Who
would not have thought, that thefe two lumi-
naries of their age had ceafed to endeavour
to grow bright by the obfcuration of each
other: yet the animadverfions thus weak, thus
precipitate, upon a book thus injured in the
tranfcription, quickly paffed the prefs; and
RELIGIO MEDICI was more accurately
published, with an admonition prefixed "to
"thofe who have or shall perufe the obferva-
"tions upon a former corrupt copy;" in
which there is a fevere cenfure, not upon
DIGBY, who was to be ufed with ceremony,
but upon the Obfervator who had ufurped
his name: nor was this invective written by
Dr. BROWNE, who was fuppofed to be fatis-
fied with his opponent's apology; but by fome
officious friend zealous for his honour, without
his confent.

BROWNE has, indeed, in his own preface,

endeavoured to fecure himfelf from rigorous examination, by alleging, that "many things "are delivered rhetorically, many expreffions "merely tropical, and therefore many things "to be taken in a foft and flexible fenfe, and "not to be called unto the rigid teft of reafon." The firft glance upon his book will indeed difcover examples of this liberty of thought and expreffion: "I could be content (fays he) "to be nothing almoft to eternity, if I might "enjoy my Saviour at the laft." He has little acquaintance with the acutenefs of BROWNE, who fufpects him of a ferious opinion, that any thing can be "almoft eternal," or that any time beginning and ending is not infinitely lefs than infinite duration.

IN this book, he fpeaks much, and, in the opinion of DIGBY, too much of himfelf; but with fuch generality and concifenefs as affords very little light to his biographer: he declares, that, befides the dialects of different provinces, he underftood fix languages; that he was no ftranger to aftronomy; and that he had feen feveral countries: but what moft awakens curiofity, is his folemn affertion, that "His life has been a miracle of thirty years; "which to relate, were not hiftory but a

"piece of poetry, and would found like a
"fable."

THERE is, undoubtedly, a fenfe, in which
all life is miraculous; as it is an union of
powers of which we can image no connexion,
a fucceffion of motions of which the firft caufe
muft be fupernatural: but life, thus explained,
whatever it may have of miracle, will have
nothing of fable; and, therefore, the author
undoubtedly had regard to fomething, by
which he imagined himfelf diftinguished
from the reft of mankind.

OF thefe wonders, however, the view that
can be now taken of his life offers no appearance. The courfe of his education was like
that of others, fuch as put him little in the way
of extraordinary cafualties. A fcholaftick and
academical life is very uniform; and has, indeed, more fafety than pleafure. A traveller
has greater opportunities of adventure; but
BROWNE traverfed no unknown feas, or
Arabian defarts: and, furely, a man may
vifit France and Italy, refide at Montpellier
and Padua, and at laft take his degree at
Leyden, without any thing miraculous. What
it was, that would, if it was related, found fo
poetical and fabulous, we are left to guefs;

I believe, without hope of gueffing rightly. The wonders probably were tranfacted in his own mind: felf-love, co-operating with an imagination vigorous and fertile as that of BROWNE, will find or make objects of aftonishment in every man's life: and, perhaps, there is no human being, however hid in the crowd from the obfervation of his fellow-mortals, who, if he has leifure and difpofition to recollect his own thoughts and actions, will not conclude his life in fome fort a miracle, and imagine himfelf diftinguished from all the reft of his fpecies by many difcriminations of nature or of fortune.

THE fuccefs of this performance was fuch, as might naturally encourage the author to new undertakings. A gentleman of Cambridge, [a] whofe name was MERRYWEATHER, turned it not inelegantly into Latin; and from his verfion it was again translated into Italian, German, Dutch, and French; and at Strafburg the Latin translation was published with large notes, by Lenuus Nicolaus Moltfarius. Of the English annotations, which in all the editions from MDCXLIV accompany the book, the author is unknown.

[a] Life of Sir THOMAS BROWNE.

OF MERRYWEATHER, to whofe zeal BROWNE was fo much indebted for the fudden extenfion of his renown, I know nothing, but that he published a fmall treatife for the inftruction of young perfons in the attainment of a Latin ftile. He printed his translation in Holland with fome difficulty [a]. The firft printer to whom he offered it, carried it to SALMASIUS, "who laid it by " (fays he) in ftate for three months," and then difcouraged its publication: it was afterwards rejected by two other printers, and at laft was received by HACKIUS.

THE peculiarities of this book raifed the author, as is ufual, many admirers and many enemies; but we know not of more than one profeffed anfwer, written under [b] the title of "Medicus medicatus," by ALEXANDER ROSS, which was universally neglected by the world.

AT the time when this book was published, Dr. BROWNE refided at Norwich, where he had fettled in MDCXXXVI, by [c] the perfuafion

[a] MERRYWEATHER's letter, inferted in the life of Sir THOMAS BROWNE.

[b] Life of Sir THOMAS BROWNE.

[c] WOOD's Athenæ Oxonienfes.

14

of Dr. LUSHINGTON his tutor, who was then rector of Barnham Weftgate in the neighbourhood. It is recorded by WOOD, that his practice was very extenfive, and that many patients reforted to him. In MDCXXXVII [a] he was incorporated Doctor of phyfick in Oxford.

HE married in MDCXLI [b] Mrs. MILEHAM, of a good family in Norfolk; "a lady (fays "WHITEFOOT) of fuch fymmetrical propor-"tion to her worthy husband, both in the "graces of her body and mind, that they "feemed to come together by a kind of "natural magnetifm."

THIS marriage could not but draw the raillery of contemporary wits [c] upon a man, who had juft been wishing in his new book, "that we might procreate, like trees, without "conjunction;" and had [d] lately declared, that "the whole world was made for man, "but only the twelfth part of man for woman;" and, that "man is the whole world, but "woman only the rib or crooked part of man."

WHETHER the lady had been yet informed of thefe contemptuous pofitions, or whether she was pleafed with the conqueft of fo

[a] WOOD.   [b] WHITEFOOT.
[c] HOWEL's letters. [d] RELIGIO MEDICI.

15

formidable a rebel, and confidered it as a double triumph, to attract fo much merit, and overcome fo powerful prejudices; or whether, like moft others, she married upon mingled motives, between convenience and inclination; she had, however, no reafon to repent: for she lived happily with him one and forty years; and bore him ten children, of whom one fon and three daughters outlived their parents: she furvived him two years, and paffed her widowhood in plenty, if not in opulence.

BROWNE having now entered the world as an author, and experienced the delights of praife and moleftations of cenfure, probably found his dread of the publick eye diminished; and, therefore, was not long before he trufted his name to the criticks a fecond time: for in MDCXLVI [a] he printed ENQUIRIES INTO VULGAR AND COMMON ERRORS; a work, which as it arofe not from fancy and invention, but from obfervation and books, and contained not a fingle difcourfe of one continued tenor, of which the latter part rofe from the former, but an enumeration of many unconnected particulars, muft have been the

[a] Life of Sir THOMAS BROWNE.

collection of years, and the effect of a defign early formed and long perfued, to which his remarks had been continually referred, and which arofe gradually to its prefent bulk by the daily aggregation of new particles of knowledge. It is, indeed, to be wished, that he had longer delayed the publication, and added what the remaining part of his life might have furnished: the thirty-fix years which he fpent afterwards in ftudy and ex- perience, would doubtlefs have made large additions to an "Enquiry into vulgar errors." He published in MDCLXXIII the fixth edition, with fome improvements; but I think rather with explications of what he had already written, than any new heads of difquifition. But with the work, fuch as the author, whether hindered from continuing it by eagernefs of praife, or wearinefs of labour, thought fit to give, we muft be content; and remember, that in all fublunary things, there is fomething to be wished, which we muft wish in vain.

THIS book, like his former, was received with great applaufe, was anfwered by ALEXANDER ROSS, and translated into Dutch and German, and not many years ago

into French. It might now be proper, had
not the favour with which it was at firſt
received filled the kingdom with copies, to
reprint it with notes partly ſupplemental and
partly emendatory, to ſubjoin thoſe diſcoveries
which the induſtry of the laſt age has made,
and correct thoſe miſtakes which the author
has committed not by idleneſs or negligence,
but for want of BOYLE's and NEWTON's
philoſophy.

HE appears, indeed, to have been willing
to pay labour for truth. Having heard a
flying rumour of ſympathetick needles, by
which, ſuſpended over a circular alphabet,
diſtant friends or lovers might correſpond, he
procured two ſuch alphabets to be made,
touched his needles with the ſame magnet,
and placed them upon proper ſpindles: the
reſult was, that when he moved one of his
needles, the other, inſtead of taking by
ſympathy the ſame direction, "ſtood like the
"pillars of Hercules." That it continued
motionleſs, will be eaſily believed; and moſt
men would have been content to believe it,
without the labour of ſo hopeleſs an experiment. BROWNE might himſelf have obtained the ſame conviction by a method leſs

operofe, if he had thruſt his needles through corks, and then ſet them afloat in two baſons of water.

NOTWITHSTANDING his zeal to detect old errors, he ſeems not very eaſy to admit new poſitions; for he never mentions the motion of the earth but with contempt and ridicule, though the opinion, which admits it, was then growing popular, and was, ſurely, plauſible, even before it was confirmed by later obſervations.

THE reputation of BROWNE encouraged ſome low writer to publish, under his name, a book called [a] "Nature's cabinet unlocked," translated, according to WOOD, from the phyſicks of MAGIRUS; of which BROWNE took care to clear himſelf, by modeſtly advertiſing, that "if any man [b] had been bene-"fited by it, he was not ſo ambitious as to "challenge the honour thereof, as having no "hand in that work."

IN MDCLVIII the diſcovery of ſome antient urns in Norfolk gave him occaſion to write HYDRIOTAPHIA, URNBURIAL, OR A DIS-COURSE OF SEPULCHRAL URNS, in which

[a] WOOD, and Life of THOMAS BROWNE.
[b] At the end of Hydriotaphia.

he treats with his ufual learning on the
funeral rites of the antient nations; exhibits
their various treatment of the dead; and ex-
amines the fubftances found in his Norfolcian
urns. There is, perhaps, none of his works
which better exemplifies his reading or
memory. It is fcarcely to be imagined, how
many particulars he has amaffed together, in
a treatife which feems to have been occafion-
ally written; and for which, therefore, no
materials could have been previously collected. It is, indeed, like other treatifes of
antiquity, rather for curiofity than ufe; for it
is of fmall importance to know which nation
buried their dead in the ground, which threw
them into the fea, or which gave them to
birds and beafts; when the practice of crema-
tion began, or when it was difufed; whether
the bones of different perfons were mingled
in the fame urn; what oblations were thrown
into the pyre; or how the ashes of the body
were diftinguished from those of other fubftances. Of the ufelefnefs of all thefe enquiries, BROWNE feems not to have been
ignorant; and, therefore, concludes them
with an obfervation which can never be too
frequently recollected.

"ALL or moſt apprehenſions reſted in
"opinions of ſome future being, which ignor-
"antly or coldly believed, begat thoſe per-
"verted conceptions, ceremonies, ſayings,
"which chriſtians pity or laugh at. Happy
"are they, which live not in that diſadvantage
"of time, when men could ſay little for futurity,
"but from reaſon; whereby the nobleſt mind
"fell often upon doubtful deaths, and melan-
"choly diſſolutions: with theſe hopes SOCRA-
"TES warmed his doubtful ſpirits, againſt the
"cold potion; and CATO, before he durſt
"give the fatal ſtroke, ſpent part of the night
"in reading the Immortality of PLATO,
"thereby confirming his wavering hand unto
"the animoſity of that attempt.

"IT is the heavieſt ſtone that melancholy
"can throw at man, to tell him he is at the
"end of his nature; or that there is no further
"ſtate to come, unto which this ſeems pro-
"greſſional, and otherwiſe made in vain:
"without this accompliſhment, the natural
"expectation and deſire of ſuch a ſtate, were
"but a fallacy in nature; unſatisfied conſide-
"rators would quarrel the juſtice of their
"conſtitution, and reſt content that ADAM
"had fallen lower, whereby, by knowing no

21

"other original, and deeper ignorance of
"themfelves, they might have enjoyed the
"happinefs of inferior creatures, who in tran-
"quillity poffefs their conftitutions, as having
"not the apprehenfion to deplore their own
"natures; and being framed below the cir-
"cumference of thefe hopes or cognition of
"better things, the wifdom of GOD hath
"neceffitated their contentment. But the
"fuperior ingredient and obfcured part of
"ourfelves, whereto all prefent felicities
"afford no refting contentment, will be able
"at laft to tell us we are more than our prefent
"felves; and evacuate fuch hopes in the
"fruition of their own accomplishments."

To his treatife on URNBURIAL was added
THE GARDEN OF CYRUS, OR THE QUIN-
CUNXIAL LOZENGE, OR NETWORK PLAN-
TATION OF THE ANTIENTS, ARTIFICIALLY,
NATURALLY, MYSTICALLY CONSIDERED.
This difcourfe he begins with the SACRED
GARDEN, in which the firft man was placed;
and deduces the practice of horticulture from
the earlieft accounts of antiquity to the time
of the Perfian CYRUS, the firft man whom
we actually know to have planted a Quin-
cunx; which, however, our author is inclined

to believe of longer date, and not only dif-
covers it in the defcription of the hanging
gardens of Babylon, but feems willing to
believe, and to perfuade his reader, that it
was practifed by the feeders on vegetables
before the flood.

SOME of the moft pleafing performances
have been produced by learning and genius
exercifed upon fubjects of little importance.
It feems to have been, in all ages, the pride
of wit, to shew how it could exalt the low,
and amplify the little. To fpeak not inade-
quately of things really and naturally great,
is a task not only difficult but difagreeable;
becaufe the writer is degraded in his own
eyes by ftanding in comparifon with his
fubject, to which he can hope to add nothing
from his imagination: but it is a perpetual
triumph of fancy to expand a fcanty theme,
to raife glittering ideas from obfcure properties, and to produce to the world an object
of wonder to which nature had contributed
little. To this ambition, perhaps, we owe the
Frogs of HOMER, the Gnat and the Bees of
VIRGIL, the Butterfly of SPENSER, the
Shadow of WOWERUS, and the Quincunx of
BROWNE.

In the profecution of this fport of fancy, he confiders every production of art and nature, in which he could find any decuffation or approaches to the form of a Quincunx; and as a man once refolved upon ideal difcoveries, feldom fearches long in vain, he finds his favourite figure in almoft every thing, whether natural or invented, antient or modern, rude or artificial, facred and civil; fo that a reader, not watchful againft the power of his infufions, would imagine that decuffation was the great bufinefs of the world, and that nature and art had no other purpofe than to exemplify and imitate a Quincunx.

To shew the excellence of this figure, he enumerates all its properties; and finds in it almoft every thing of ufe or pleafure: and to shew how readily he fupplies what he cannot find, one inftance may be fufficient; "though "therein (fays he) we meet not with right "angles, yet every rhombus containing four "angles equal unto two right, it virtually "contains two right in every one."

The fanciful fports of great minds are never without fome advantage to knowledge. Browne has interfperfed many curious obfervations on the form of plants, and the laws

24

of vegetation; and appears to have been a very accurate obferver of the modes of germination, and to have watched with great nicety the evolution of the parts of plants from their feminal principles.

He is then naturally led to treat of the number five; and finds, that by this number many things are circumfcribed; that there are five kinds of vegetable productions, five fections of a cone, five orders of architecture, and five acts of a play. And obferving that five was the antient conjugal or wedding number, he proceeds to a fpeculation which I shall give in his own words; "The antient "numerifts made out the conjugal number by "two and three, the firft parity and imparity, "the active and paffive digits, the material "and formal principles in generative focie-"ties."

These are all the tracts which he published: but many papers were found in his clofet, "Some of them, (fays Whitefoot) defigned "for the prefs, were often tranfcribed and "corrected by his own hand, after the fashion "of great and curious writers."

Of thefe, two collections have been published; one by Dr. Tennison, the other

in MDCCXXII by a namelefs editor. Whether
the one or the other felected thofe pieces
which the author would have preferred,
cannot now be known: but they have both
the merit of giving to mankind what was
too valuable to be fuppreffed; and what
might, without their interpofition, have,
perhaps, perished among other innumer-
able labours of learned men, or have been
burnt in a fcarcity of fuel like the papers of
Pereskius.

THE firft of thefe pofthumous treatifes
contains "Obfervations upon feveral plants
"mentioned in Scripture." Thefe remarks,
though they do not immediately either rectify
the faith, or refine the morals of the reader,
yet are by no means to be cenfured as fuperfluous niceties or ufelefs fpeculations; for
they often shew fome propriety of defcription, or elegance of allufion, utterly un-
difcoverable to readers not skilled in oriental
botany; and are often of more important ufe,
as they remove fome difficulty from narra-
tives, or fome obfcurity from precepts.

THE next is "Of garlands, or coronary and
"garland plants;" a fubject merely of learned
curiofity, without any other end than the

pleafure of reflecting on antient cuftoms, or on the induftry with which ftudious men have endeavoured to recover them.

THE next is a letter, "on the fishes eaten "by our SAVIOUR with his difciples, after "his refurrection from the dead;" which contains no determinate refolution of the queftion, what they were, for indeed it cannot be determined. All the information that diligence or learning could fupply, confifts in an enumeration of the fishes produced in the waters of Judea.

THEN follow "Anfwers to certain queries "about fishes, birds, and infects;" and "A "letter of hawks and falconry antient and "modern:" in the firft of which he gives the proper interpretation of fome antient names of animals, commonly miftaken; and in the other has fome curious obfervations on the art of hawking, which he confiders as a practice unknown to the antients. I believe all our fports of the field are of Gothick original; the antients neither hunted by the fcent, nor feem much to have practifed horfe-manship as an exercife; and though, in their works, there is mention of "aucupium" and "pifcatio," they feem no more to have been confidered as diverfions, than agriculture or any other manual labour.

In two more letters he fpeaks of "the cym-"bals of the Hebrews," but without any fatisfactory determination; and of "repalick "or gradual verfes," that is, of verfes begin-ning with a word of one fyllable, and pro-ceeding by words of which each has a fyllable more than the former; as,

O Deus, æternæ ftationis conciliator.
AUSONIUS.

and, after his manner, purfuing the hint, he mentions many other reftrained methods of verfifying, to which induftrious ignorance has fometimes voluntarily fubjected itfelf.

His next attempt is "On languages, and "particularly the Saxon tongue." He dif-courfes with great learning, and generally with great juftnefs, of the derivation and changes of languages; but, like other men of multifarious learning, he receives fome no-tions without examination. Thus he obferves, according to the popular opinion, that the Spaniards have retained fo much Latin, as to be able to compofe fentences that shall be at once gramatically Latin and Caftilian:

this will appear very unlikely to a man that confiders the Spanish terminations; and HOWEL, who was eminently skilful in the three provincial languages, declares, that after many effays he never could effect it.

THE principal defign of this letter, is to shew the affinity between the modern English and the antient Saxon; and he obferves, very rightly, that "though we have borrowed "many fubftantives, adjectives, and fome "verbs, from the French; yet the great body "of numerals, auxiliary verbs, articles, pro- "nouns, adverbs, conjunctions, and prepofi- "tions, which are the diftinguishing and "lafting parts of a language, remain with us "from the Saxon."

To prove this pofition more evidently, he has drawn up a short difcourfe of fix para- graphs, in Saxon and English; of which every word is the fame in both languages, excepting the terminations and orthography. The words are, indeed, Saxon, but the phrafeology is English; and, I think, would not have been underftood by BEDE or ÆLFRIC, notwith- ftanding the confidence of our author. He has, however, fufficiently proved his pofition, that the English refembles its parental language, more than any modern European dialect.

THERE remain five tracts of this collection yet unmentioned; one "Of artificial hills, "mounts, or burrows, in England;" in reply to an interrogatory letter of E. D. whom the writers of BIOGRAPHIA BRITANNICA suppofe to be, if rightly printed, W. D. or Sir WILLIAM DUGDALE, one of BROWNE's correfpondents. Thefe are declared by BROWNE, in concurrence, I think, with all other antiquarians, to be for the moft part funeral monuments. He proves, that both the Danes and Saxons buried their men of eminence under piles of earth, "which ad-"mitting (fays he) neither ornament, epitaph, "nor infcription, may, if earthquakes fpare "them, outlaft other monuments: obelisks "have their term, and pyramids will tumble; "but thefe mountainous monuments may "ftand, and are like to have the fame period "with the earth."

IN the next, he anfwers two geographical queftions; one concerning Troas, mentioned in the Acts and Epiftles of St. PAUL, which he determines to be the city built near the antient Ilium; and the other concerning the

dead fea, of which he gives the fame account
with other writers.

ANOTHER letter treats "Of the anfwers of
"the oracle of Apollo at Delphos, to Crœfus
"king of Lydia." In this tract nothing de-
ferves notice, more than that BROWNE confiders the oracles as evidently and indubitably
fupernatural, and founds all his difquifition
upon that poftulate. He wonders why the
phyfiologifts of old, having fuch means of
inftruction, did not inquire into the fecrets of
nature: but judiciously concludes, that fuch
queftions would probably have been vain;
"for, in matters cognofcible, and formed for
"our difquifition, our induftry muft be our
"oracle, and reafon our Apollo."

THE pieces that remain are, "A prophecy
"concerning the future ftate of feveral
"nations;" in which BROWNE plainly dif-
covers his expectation to be the fame with
that entertained lately with more confidence
by Dr. BERKLEY, "that America will be the
"feat of the fifth empire:" and "Mufeum
"claufum, five Bibliotheca abfcondita;" in
which the author amufes himfelf with im-
agining the exiftence of books and curiofities,
either never in being, or irrecoverably loft.

THESE pieces I have recounted as they are ranged in TENNISON's collection, becaufe the editor has given no account of the time at which any of them were written. Some of them are of little value, more than as they gratify the mind with the picture of a great fcholar, turning his learning into amufement; or shew, upon how great a variety of enquiries the fame mind has been fuccefsfully employed.

THE other collection of his pofthumous pieces, published in octavo, London MDCCXXII, contains "Repertorium; or fome account of "the tombs and monuments in the cathedral "of Norwich;" where, as TENNISON ob-ferves, there is not matter proportionate to the skill of the Antiquary.

THE other pieces are, "Anfwers to Sir "WILLIAM DUGDALE's enquiries about the "fens; A letter concerning Ireland; Another "relating to urns newly difcovered; Some "short ftrictures on different fubjects;" and "A letter to a friend on the death of his in-"timate friend," published fingly by the author's fon in MDCXC.

THERE is inferted, in the BIOGRAPHIA BRITANNICA, "A letter containing inftruc-"tions for the ftudy of phyfick;" which, with the Essays here offered to the public, completes the works of Dr. BROWNE.

To the life of this learned man, there remains little to be added, but that in MDCLXV he was chofen honorary fellow of the college of phyficians, as a man, "Virtute et literis "ornatiffimus,—eminently embellished with "literature and virtue:" and, in MDCLXXI, received, at Norwich, the honour of knighthood from CHARLES II; a prince, who with many frailties and vices, had yet skill to difcover excellence, and virtue to reward it, with fuch honorary diftinctions at leaft as coft him nothing, yet conferred by a king fo judicious and fo much beloved, had the power of giving merit new luftre and greater popularity.

THUS he lived in high reputation; till in his feventy-fixth year he was feized with a colick, which, after having tortured him about a week, put an end to his life at Norwich, on his birthday, October 19, MDCLXXXII. [a] Some of his laft words were expreffions of fubmiffion to the will of GOD, and fearlefnefs of death.

HE lies buried in the church of St. Peter, Mancroft, in Norwich, with this infcription

[a] BROWNE'S Remains. WHITEFOOT.

on a mural monument, placed on the fouth
pillar of the altar:

M. S.

Hic fitus eft THOMAS BROWNE, M. D.

Et Miles.

A° 1605. Londini natus
Generofa Familia apud Upton
In agro Ceftrienfi oriundus.
Scholâ primum Wintonienfi, poftea
In Coll. Pembr.
Apud Oxonienfes bonis literis
Haud leviter imbutus
In urbe hâc Nordovicenfi medicinam
Arte egregia, & fælici fucceffu profeffus,
Scriptis quibus tituli, RELIGIO MEDICI
Et PSEUDODOXIA EPIDEMICA aliifque
Per Orbem notiffimus.
Vir Prudentiffimus, Integerrimus, Doctiffimus;
Obiit Octobr. 19. 1682.
Pie pofuit mæftiffima Conjux
Da. Doroth. Br.

Near the Foot of this Pillar
Lies Sir Thomas Browne, Kt. and Doctor in Phyfick,
Author of Religio Medici, and other Learned Books,
Who practic'd Phyfick in this City 46 Years,
And died Octr. 1682, in the 77 Year of his Age.
In Memory of whom
Dame *Dorothy Browne*, who had bin his Affectionate Wife
47 Years, caufed this Monument to be Erected.

34

BESIDES his lady, who died in MDCLXXXV, he left a fon and three daughters. Of the daughters nothing very remarkable is known; but his fon, EDWARD BROWNE, requires a particular mention.

HE was born about the year MDCXLII; and after having paffed through the claffes of the fchool at Norwich, became bachelor of phyfick at Cambridge; and afterwards removing to Merton-College in Oxford, was admitted there to the fame degree, and afterwards made a doctor. In MDCLXVIII he vifited part of Germany; and in the year following made a wider excurfion into Auftria, Hungary, and Theffaly; where the Turkish Sultan then kept his court at Lariffa. He afterwards paffed through Italy. His skill in natural hiftory made him particularly attentive to mines and metallurgy. Upon his return he published an account of the countries thro' which he had paffed; which I have heard commended by a learned traveller, who has vifited many places after him, as written with fcrupulous and exact veracity, fuch as is fcarcely to be found in any other book of the fame kind. But whatever it may contribute to the inftruction of a naturalift, I cannot recommend it as likely to give much pleafure to common readers: for whether it be, that the world is very uniform, and therefore he who is refolved to adhere to truth, will have few novelties to relate; or that Dr. BROWNE was, by the train of his ftudies, led to enquire moft after thofe things, by which the greateft part of mankind is little affected; a great part of his book feems to contain very unimportant accounts of his paffage from one place where he faw little, to another where he faw no more.

UPON his return, he practifed phyfick in London; was made phyfician firft to CHARLES II, and afterwards in MDCLXXXII to St. Bartholomew's hofpital. About the fame time he joined his name to thofe of many other eminent men, in "A translation of Plutarch's "lives." He was firft cenfor, then elect, and treafurer of the college of phyficians; of which in MDCCV he was chofen prefident, and held his office, till in MDCCVIII he died in a degree of eftimation fuitable to a man fo varioufly accomplished, that King CHARLES had honoured him with this panegyrick, that "He was as learned as any of the college, and "as well-bred as any of the court."

OF every great and eminent character, part
breaks forth into publick view, and part lies
hid in domeftick privacy. Thofe qualities
which have been exerted in any known and
lafting performances, may, at any diftance of
time, be traced and eftimated; but filent excellencies are foon forgotten; and thofe minute
peculiarities which difcriminate every man
from all others, if they are not recorded by
thofe whom perfonal knowledge enabled to
obferve them, are irrecoverably loft. This
mutilation of character muft have happened,
among many others, to Sir THOMAS BROWNE,
had it not been delineated by his friend Mr.
WHITEFOOT, who "efteemed it an efpecial
"favour of PROVIDENCE, to have had a
"particular acquaintance with him for two
"thirds of his life." Part of his obfervations
I shall, therefore, copy.

"FOR a character of his perfon, his com-
"plexion and hair was anfwerable to his
"name; his ftature was moderate, and habit
"of body neither fat nor lean, but εὐσαρκ☉.
"IN his habit of clothing, he had an aver-
"fion to all finery, and affected plainnefs,
"both in the fashion and ornaments. He ever

"wore a cloke, or boots, when few others did.
"He kept himſelf always very warm, and
"thought it moſt ſafe ſo to do, though he
"never loaded himſelf with ſuch a multitude
"of garments, as Suetonius reports of Au-
"GUSTUS, enough to clothe a good family.

"THE horizon of his underſtanding was
"much larger than the hemiſphere of the
"world: All that was viſible in the heavens
"he comprehended ſo well, that few that are
"under them knew ſo much: He could tell
"the number of the viſible ſtars in his horizon,
"and call them all by their names that had
"any; and of the earth he had ſuch a minute
"and exact geographical knowledge, as if
"he had been by DIVINE PROVIDENCE
"ordained ſurveyor-general of the whole ter-
"reſtrial orb, and its products, minerals,
"plants, and animals. He was ſo curious a
"botaniſt, that beſides the ſpecifical dif-
"tinctions, he made nice and elaborate ob-
"ſervations, equally uſeful as entertaining.

"HIS memory, though not ſo eminent as
"that of SENECA or SCALIGER, was capa-
"cious and tenacious, inſomuch as he
"remembred all that was remarkable in any
"book that he had read; and not only knew

"all perfons again that he had ever feen at
"any diftance of time, but remembred the
"circumftances of their bodies, and their
"particular difcourfes and fpeeches.

"In the latin poets he remembred every
"thing that was acute and pungent; he had
"read moft of the hiftorians, antient and
"modern, wherein his obfervations were
"fingular, not taken notice of by common
"readers; he was excellent company when
"he was at leifure, and expreffed more light
"than heat in the temper of his brain.

"He had no defpotical power over his
"affections and paffions, (that was a privilege
"of original perfection, forfeited by the
"neglect of the ufe of it;) but as large a
"political power over them, as any Stoick, or
"man of his time, whereof he gave fo great
"experiment, that he hath very rarely been
"known to have been overcome with any of
"them. The ftrongeft that were found in him,
"both of the irafcible and concupifcible, were
"under the controul of his reafon. Of ad-
"miration, which is one of them, being the
"only product, either of ignorance, or un-
"common knowledge, he had more, and lefs,
"than other men, upon the fame account of

"his knowing more than others; fo that tho'
"he met with many rarities, he admired them
"not fo much as others do.

"HE was never feen to be tranfported with
"mirth, or dejected with fadnefs; always
"chearful, but rarely merry, at any fenfible
"rate; feldom heard to break a jeft; and when
"he did, he would be apt to blush at the
"levity of it: his gravity was natural without
"affectation.

"HIS modefty was vifible in a natural
"habitual blush, which was increafed upon
"the leaft occafion, and oft difcovered without
"any obfervable caufe.

"THEY that knew no more of him than
"by the brisknefs of his writings, found them-
"felves deceived in their expectation, when
"they came in his company, noting the
"gravity and fobriety of his afpect and con-
"verfation; fo free from loquacity, or much
"talkativenefs, that he was fomething diffi-
"cult to be engaged in any difcourfe; though
"when he was fo, it was always fingular, and
"never trite or vulgar. Parfimonious in
"nothing but his time, whereof he made as
"much improvement, with as little lofs as
"any man in it: when he had any to fpare

"from his drudging practice, he was scarce
"patient of any diversion from his study; so
"impatient of sloth and idleness, that he
"would say, he could not do nothing.

"Sir Thomas understood most of the
"European languages; viz. all that are in
"Hutter's bible, which he made use of.
"The Latin and Greek he understood criti-
"cally; the Oriental languages, which never
"were vernacular in this part of the world,
"he thought the use of them would not
"answer the time and pains of learning them;
"yet had so great a veneration for the matrix
"of them, viz. the Hebrew, consecrated to
"the Oracles of God, that he was not content
"to be totally ignorant of it; tho' very little
"of his science is to be found in any books of
"that primitive language. And tho' much
"is said to be written in the derivative idioms
"of that tongue, especially the Arabick, yet
"he was satisfied with the translations,
"wherein he found nothing admirable.

"In his religion he continued in the same
"mind which he had declared in his first book,
"written when he was but thirty years old,
"his Religio Medici, wherein he fully
"assented to that of the church of England,

"preferring it before any in the world, as did
"the learned GROTIUS. He attended the
"publick fervice very conftantly, when he
"was not withheld by his practice. Never
"miffed the facrament in his parish, if he
"were in town. Read the beft English
"fermons he could hear of, with liberal
"applaufe; and delighted not in controverfies.
"In his laft ficknefs, wherein he continued
"about a week's time, enduring great pain
"of the cholick, befides a continual fever,
"with as much patience as hath been feen
"in any man, without any pretence of Stoical
"apathy, animofity, or vanity of not being
"concerned thereat, or fuffering no impeach-
"ment of happinefs. Nihil agis dolor.

"His patience was founded upon the
"chriftian philofophy, and a found faith of
"God's Providence, and a meek and
"humble fubmiffion thereunto, which he ex-
"preffed in few words: I vifited him near his
"end, when he had not ftrength to hear or
"fpeak much; the laft words which I heard
"from him, were, befides fome expreffions of
"dearnefs, that he did freely fubmit to the
"will of God, being without fear: He had oft
"triumphed over the king of terrors in others,

"and given many repulſes in the defence of
"patients; but when his own turn came, he
"ſubmitted with a meek, rational, and re-
"ligious courage.

"HE might have made good the old ſaying
"of Dat Galenus opes, had he lived in a place
"that could have afforded it. But his in-
"dulgence and liberality to his children,
"eſpecially in their travels, two of his ſons in
"divers countries, and two of his daughters
"in France, ſpent him more than a little.
"He was liberal in his houſe entertainments,
"and in his charity; he left a comfortable,
"but no great eſtate, both to his lady and
"children, gained by his own induſtry.

"SUCH was his ſagacity and knowledge of
"all hiſtory, antient and modern, and his
"obſervations thereupon ſo ſingular, that it
"hath been ſaid by them that knew him beſt,
"that if his profeſſion, and place of abode,
"would have ſuited his ability, he would have
"made an extraordinary man for the privy-
"council, not much inferior to the famous
"PADRE, PAULO, the late oracle of the
"Venetian ſtate.

"THO' he were no prophet, nor ſon of a
"prophet, yet in that faculty which comes

43

"neareſt it, he excelled, *i.e.* the ſtochaſtick,
"wherein he was ſeldom miſtaken, as to
"future events, as well publick as private;
"but not apt to diſcover any preſages or
"ſuperſtition."

IT is obſervable, that he who in his earlier
years had read all the books againſt religion,
was in the latter part of his life averſe from
controverſies. To play with important truths,
to diſturb the repoſe of eſtablished tenets, to
ſubtilize objections, and elude proof, is too
often the ſport of youthful vanity, of which
maturer experience commonly repents. There
is a time, when every wiſe man is weary of
raiſing difficulties only to task himſelf with
the ſolution, and deſires to enjoy truth without the labour or hazard of conteſt. There is,
perhaps, no better method of encountering
theſe troubleſome irruptions of ſcepticiſm,
with which inquiſitive minds are frequently
harraſſed, than that which BROWNE declares
himſelf to have taken: "If there ariſe any
"doubts in my way, I do forget them; or at
"leaſt defer them, till my better ſettled judg-
"ment and more manly reaſon be able to
"reſolve them: for I perceive, every man's
"reaſon is his beſt OEDIPUS, and will, upon

"a reafonable truce, find a way to loofe thofe
"bonds, wherewith the fubtilties of error
"have enchained our more flexible and tender
"judgments."

THE foregoing character may be confirmed
and enlarged, by many paffages in the RE-
LIGIO MEDICI; in which it appears, from
WHITEFOOT's teftimony, that the author,
though no very fparing panegyrift of himfelf,
has not exceeded the truth, with refpect to
his attainments or vifible qualities.

THERE are, indeed, fome interior and
fecret virtues, which a man may fometimes
have without the knowledge of others; and
may fometimes affume to himfelf, without
fufficient reafons for his opinion. It is
charged upon BROWNE by Dr. WATTS, as
an inftance of arrogant temerity, that, after
a long detail of his attainments, he declares
himfelf to have efcaped "the firft and father-
"fin of pride." A perufal of the RELIGIO
MEDICI will not much contribute to produce
a belief of the author's exemption from this
FATHER-SIN: pride is a vice, which pride
itfelf inclines every man to find in others, and
to overlook in himfelf.

As eafily may we be miftaken in eftimating

our own courage, as our own humility; and, therefore, when BROWNE shews himſelf perſuaded, that "he could loſe an arm without "a tear, or with a few groans be quartered to "pieces," I am not ſure that he felt in himſelf any uncommon powers of endurance; or, indeed, any thing more than a ſudden efferv
eſcence of imagination, which, uncertain and involuntary as it is, he miſtook for ſettled reſolution.

"THAT there were not many extant, that "in a noble way feared the face of death leſs "than himſelf," he might likewiſe believe at a very eaſy expence, while death was yet at a diſtance; but the time will come to every human being, when it muſt be known how well he can bear to die; and it has appeared, that our author's fortitude did not deſert him in the great hour of trial.

IT was obſerved by ſome of the remarkers on the RELIGIO MEDICI, that "the author "was yet alive, and might grow worſe as well "as better:" it is, therefore, happy, that this ſuſpicion can be obviated by a teſtimony given to the continuance of his virtue, at a time when death had ſet him free from danger of change, and his panegyriſt from temptation to flattery.

But it is not on the praifes of others, but on his own writings, that he is to depend for the efteem of pofterity; of which he will not eafily be deprived, while learning shall have any reverence among men: for there is no fcience, in which he does not difcover fome skill; and fcarce any kind of knowledge, profane or facred, abftrufe or elegant, which he does not appear to have cultivated with fuccefs.

His exuberance of knowledge, and plenitude of ideas, fometimes obftruct the tendency of his reafoning, and the clearnefs of his decifions: on whatever fubject he employed his mind, there ftarted up immediately fo many images before him, that he loft one by grafping another. His memory fupplied him with fo many illuftrations, parallel or dependent notions, that he was always ftarting into collateral confiderations: but the fpirit and vigour of his perfuit always gives delight; and the reader follows him, without reluctance, thro' his mazes, in themfelves flowery and pleafing, and ending at the point originally in view.

To have great excellencies, and great faults, "magnæ virtutes nec minora vitia, is

"the poefy," fays our author, "of the beft
"natures." This poefy may be properly applied to the ftyle of BROWNE: It is vigorous,
but rugged; it is learned, but pedantick; it is
deep, but obfcure; it ftrikes, but does not
pleafe; it commands, but does not allure: his
tropes are harsh, and his combinations un-
couth. He fell into an age, in which our language began to lofe the ftability which it had
obtained in the time of ELIZABETH; and was
confidered by every writer as a fubject on
which he might try his plaftick skill, by
moulding it according to his own fancy.
MILTON, in confequence of this encroaching
licence, began to introduce the Latin idiom:
and BROWNE, though he gave lefs difturb-
ance to our ftructures and phrafeology, yet
poured in a multitude of exotick words;
many, indeed, ufeful and fignificant, which,
if rejected, muft be fupplied by circumlocu-
tion, fuch as COMMENSALITY for the ftate of
many living at the fame table; but many
fuperfluous, as a PARALOGICAL for an un-
reafonable doubt; and fome fo obfcure, that
they conceal his meaning rather than explain
it, as ARTHRITICAL ANALOGIES for parts
that ferve fome animals in the place of joints.

48

His ftyle is, indeed, a tiffue of many lán-
guages; a mixture of heterogeneous words,
brought together from diftant regions, with
terms originally appropriated to one art, and
drawn by violence into the fervice of another.
He muft, however, be confeffed to have
augmented our philofophical diction; and in
defence of his uncommon words and expreffions, we muft confider, that he had
uncommon fentiments, and was not content
to exprefs in many words that idea for
which any language could fupply a fingle
term.

But his innovations are fometimes pleafing,
and his temerities happy: he has many
"verba ardentia," forcible expreffions, which
he would never have found, but by venturing
to the utmoft verge of propriety; and flights
which would never have been reached, but
by one who had very little fear of the shame
of falling.

THERE remains yet an objection againft
the writings of BROWNE, more formidable
than the animadverfions of criticifm. There
are paffages, from which fome have taken
occafion to rank him among Deifts, and
others among Atheifts. It would be difficult

to guefs how any fuch conclufion should be formed, had not experience shewn that there are two forts of men willing to enlarge the catalogue of infidels.

IT has been long obferved, that an Atheift has no juft reafon for endeavouring converfions; and yet none harrafs thofe minds which they can influence, with more importunity of folicitation to adopt their opinions. In proportion as they doubt the truth of their own doctrines, they are defirous to gain the atteftation of another underftanding; and induftriously labour to win a profelyte, and eagerly catch at the slighteft pretence to dignify their fect with a celebrated name*.

THE others become friends to infidelity only by unfkilful hoftility: men of rigid orthodoxy, cautious converfation, and religious afperity. Among thefe, it is too frequently the practice, to make in their heat conceffions to Atheifm, or Deifm, which their

* Therefore no hereticks defire to fpread
  Their wild opinions like thefe epicures.
  For fo their ftagg'ring thoughts are computed,
  And other men's affent their doubt affures.
                                        DAVIES.

moſt confident advocates had never dared to claim or to hope. A ſally of levity, an idle paradox, an indecent jeſt, an unſeaſonable objection, are ſufficient, in the opinion of theſe men, to efface a name from the liſts of CHRISTIANITY, to exclude a ſoul from ever-laſting life. Such men are ſo watchful to cenſure, that they have ſeldom much care to look for favourable interpretations of am-biguities, to ſet the general tenor of life againſt ſingle failures, or to know how ſoon any ſlip of inadvertency has been expiated by ſorrow and retractation; but let fly their fulminations, without mercy or prudence, againſt ſlight offences or caſual temerities, againſt crimes never committed, or immedi-ately repented.

THE Infidel knows well, what he is doing. He is endeavouring to ſupply, by authority, the deficiency of his arguments; and to make his cauſe leſs invidious, by ſhewing numbers on his ſide: he will, therefore, not change his conduct, till he reforms his principles. But the zealot ſhould recollect, that he is labour-ing, by this frequency of excommunication, againſt his own cauſe; and voluntarily adding ſtrength to the enemies of truth. It muſt always be the condition of a great part of mankind, to reject and embrace tenets upon the authority of those whom they think wifer than themfelves; and, therefore, the addition of every name to infidelity, in fome degree invalidates that argument upon which the religion of multitudes is neceffarily founded.

MEN may differ from each other in many religious opinions, and yet all may retain the effentials of CHRISTIANITY; men may fometimes eagerly difpute, and yet not differ much from one another: the rigorous perfecutors of error, should, therefore, enlighten their zeal with knowledge, and temper their orthodoxy with CHARITY; that CHARITY, without which orthodoxy is vain; CHARITY that "thinketh no evil," but "hopeth all things," and "endureth all things."

WHETHER BROWNE has been numbered among the contemners of religion, by the fury of its friends, or the artifice of its enemies, it is no difficult task to replace him among the moft zealous PROFESSORS of CHRISTIANITY. He may, perhaps, in the ardour of his imagination, have hazarded an expreffion, which a mind intent upon

faults may interpret into herefy, if confidered
apart from the reſt of his difcourfe; but a
phrafe is not to be oppofed to volumes: there
is fcarcely a writer to be found, whofe profeſſion was not divinity, that has fo frequently
teſtified his belief of the SACRED WRITINGS,
has appealed to them with fuch unlimited
fubmiſſion, or mentioned them with fuch
unvaried reverence.

ITis, indeed, fomewhat wonderful, that HE
should be placed without the pale of CHRIS-
TIANITY, who declares, that "he aſſumes the
"honourable ſtile of A CHRISTIAN," not
becaufe it is "the religion of his country,"
but becaufe "having in his riper years and
"confirmed judgment feen and examined all,
"he finds himſelf obliged, by the principles of
"GRACE, and the law of his own reafon, to
"embrace no other name but this:" Who, to
fpecify his perfuafion yet more, tells us, that
"he is of the REFORMED RELIGION; of
"the fame belief our SAVIOUR taught, the
"APOSTLES diſſeminated, the Fathers au-
"thorized, and the Martyrs confirmed:"
Who, tho' "paradoxical in philofophy, loves
"in divinity to keep the beaten road;" and
pleafes himſelf, that "he has no taint of

"herefy, fchifm, or error:" To whom "where
"the Scripture is filent, the Church is a text;
"where that fpeaks, 'tis but a comment;"
and who ufes not "the dictates of his own
"reafon, but where there is a joint filence of
"both:" Who "bleffes himfelf, that he lived
"not in the days of miracles, when faith had
"been thruft upon him; but enjoys that
"greater bleffing, pronounced to all that
"believe and faw not." He cannot furely be
charged with a defect of faith, who "believes
"that our SAVIOUR was dead, and buried,
"and rofe again, and defires to fee him in his
"glory:" and who affirms, that "this is not
"much to believe;" that "as we have reafon,
"we owe this faith unto hiftory;" and that
"they only had the advantage of a bold and
"noble faith, who lived before his coming;
"and, upon obfcure prophecies and myftical
"types, could raife a belief." Nor can contempt of the pofitive and ritual parts of religion be imputed to him, who doubts,
whether a good man would refufe a poifoned
eucharift; and "who would violate his own
"arm, rather than a church."

THE opinions of every man muft be
learned from himfelf: concerning his practice,

it is fafeſt to truſt the evidence of others. Where theſe teſtimonies concur, no higher degree of hiſtorical certainty can be obtained; and they apparently concur to prove, that BROWNE was A ZEALOUS ADHERENT TO THE FAITH OF CHRIST, that HE LIVED IN OBEDIENCE TO HIS LAWS, AND DIED IN CONFIDENCE OF HIS MERCY.

CHRISTIAN MORALS

BY

SIR THOMAS BROWNE
Kt., M.D.

To the

RIGHT HONOURABLE

DAVID EARL OF BUCHAN,

VISCOUNT AUCHTERHÓUSE, LORD CARDROSS
AND GLENDOVACHIE,
ONE OF THE LORDS COMMISSIONERS OF POLICE,
AND LORD LIEUTENANT OF THE COUNTIES OF
STIRLING AND CLACKMANNAN IN
NORTH BRITAIN

My Lord,

THE Honour you have done our Family obligeth us to make all juſt Acknowledgments of it: and there is no Form of Acknowledgment in our Power, more worthy of Your Lordship's Acceptance, than this Dedication of the laſt Work of our Honoured and Learned Father. Encouraged hereunto by the Knowledge we have of Your Lordship's Judicious Relish of univerſal Learning, and ſublime Virtue, we beg the Favour of Your Acceptance of it, which will very much oblige our Family in general, and Her in particular, who is,

My Lord,

Your Lordship's

moſt humble Servant,

ELIZABETH LITTLETON.

THE PREFACE

If any one, after he has read Religio Medici, *and the enſuing Diſcourſe, can make doubt, whether the ſame perſon was the author of them both, he may be aſſured by the teſtimony of Mrs.* LITTLETON, *Sir* THOMAS BROWN's *daughter, who lived with her father when it was compoſed by him; and who, at the time, read it written by his own hand: and alſo by the teſtimony of others, (of whom I am one) who read the manuſcript of the author, immediately after his death, and who have ſince read the ſame; from which it hath been faithfully and exactly tranſcribed for the preſs. The reaſon why it was not printed ſooner is, becauſe it was unhappily loſt, by being mislay'd among other manuſcripts for which ſearch was lately made in the preſence of the Lord Arch-biſhop of Canterbury, of which his Grace, by letter, informed Mrs.* LITTLETON, *when he ſent the manuſcript to her. There is nothing printed in the diſcourſe, or in the short notes, but what is found in the original manuſcript of the author, except only where an overſight had made the addition or tranſ-poſition of ſome words neceſſary.*

JOHN JEFFERY,
Arch-Deacon of Norwich.

CHRISTIAN MORALS

PART ONE

§ 1

TREAD foftly and circumfpectly in this ᵃ funambulatory track and narrow path of goodnefs: purfue virtue virtuoufly: leven not good actions, nor render virtues difputable. Stain not fair acts with foul intentions: maim not uprightnefs by halting concomitances, nor circumftantially deprave fubftantial goodnefs.

CONSIDER whereabout thou art in ᵇ CEBES's table, or that old philofophical ᶜ pinax of the life of man: whether thou

ᵃ Narrow, like the walk of a rope-dancer.

ᵇ The table or picture of CEBES, an allegorical reprefentation of the characters and conditions of mankind; which is translated by Mr. Collier, and added to the meditations of ANTONINUS.

ᶜ Picture.

art yet in the road of uncertainties;
whether thou haſt yet entred the narrow
gate, got up the hill and aſperous way,
which leadeth unto the houſe of ſanity;
or taken that purifying potion from the
hand of ſincere erudition, which may
ſend thee clear and pure away unto a
virtuous and happy life.

IN this virtuous voyage of thy life hull
not about like the ark, without the uſe
of rudder, maſt, or ſail, and bound for no
port. Let not diſappointment cauſe deſ-
pondency, nor difficulty deſpair. Think
not that you are ſailing from a Lima to
Manillia, when you may faſten up the
rudder, and sleep before the wind; but
expeſt rough ſeas, b flaws, and contrary
blaſts: and 'tis well, if by many croſs tacks
and veerings you arrive at the port; for

a Over the pacifick ocean, in the courſe of the ship
which now ſails from Acapulco to Manilla, perhaps
formerly from Lima, or more properly from Callao,
Lima not being a ſea-port.
b "Sudden guſts, or violent attacks of bad weather."

64

we sleep in [a] lions' skins in our progress unto virtue, and we slide not but climb unto it.

SIT not down in the popular forms and common level of virtues. Offer not only peace-offerings but holocausts unto GOD: where all is due make no reserve, and cut not a cummin-seed with the AL-MIGHTY: to serve Him singly to serve ourselves, were too partial a piece of piety; not like to place us in the illustrious mansions of glory.

§ 2

REST not in an [b] ovation but a triumph over thy passions. Let anger walk hanging down the head; let malice go manicled, and envy fetter'd after thee. Behold within thee the long train of thy

[a] That is, "in armour, in a state of military vigi-"lance." One of the Grecian chiefs used to represent open force by the "lion's skin," and policy by the "fox's tail."

[b] Ovation, a petty and minor kind of triumph. *Note to the first edition.*

trophies, not without thee. ᵃ Make the quarrelling Lapithytes sleep, and Centaurs within lie quiet. Chain up the unruly legion of thy breaſt. Lead thine own captivity captive, and be Cæſar within thyſelf.

§ 3

HE that is chaſt and continent not to impair his ſtrength, or honeſt for fear of contagion, will hardly be heroically virtuous. Adjourn not this virtue until that temper, when ᵇ Cato could lend out his wife, and impotent ſatyrs write ſatyrs upon luſt: but be chaſt in thy flaming days, when Alexander dar'd not truſt his eyes upon the fair ſiſters of Darius, and when ſo many think there is no other way but ᶜ Origen's.

ᵃ That is, "thy turbulent and iraſcible paſſions." For the Lapithytes and Centaurs, ſee Ovid.

ᵇ The Cenſor, who is frequently confounded, and by POPE amongſt others, with Cato of Utica.

ᶜ Who is ſaid to have caſtrated himſelf. *Note to the firſt edition.*

§ 4

SHOW thy art in honefty, and lofe not thy virtue by the bad managery of it. Be temperate and fober; not to preferve your body in an ability for wanton ends; not to avoid the infamy of common tranfgreffors that way, and thereby to hope to expiate or palliate obfcure and clofer vices; not to fpare your purfe, nor fimply to enjoy health: but in one word, that thereby you may truly ferve GOD, which every ficknefs will tell you you cannot well do without health. The fick man's facrifice is but a lame oblation. Pious treafures laid up in healthful days, plead for fick non-performances: without which we muft needs look back with anxiety upon the loft opportunities of health; and may have caufe rather to envy than pity the ends of penitent publick fufferers, who go with healthful prayers unto the laft fcene of their lives, and [a] in the integrity of their faculties return their fpirit unto GOD that gave it.

§ 5

BE charitable before wealth make thee covetous, and lofe not the glory of the mite. If riches increafe, let thy mind hold pace with them; and think it not enough to be liberal, but munificent. Though a cup of cold water from fome hand may not be without its reward, yet ftick not thou for wine and oil for the wounds of the diftreffed; and treat the poor, as our SAVIOUR did the multitude, to the reliques of fome baskets. Diffufe thy beneficence early, and while thy treafures call thee mafter: there may be an [b] Atropos of thy fortunes before that of thy life, and thy wealth cut off before that hour, when all men shall be poor; for the juftice of death looks equally upon

[a] "With their faculties unimpaired."

[b] Atropos is the lady of deftiny that cuts the thread of life.

the dead, and Charon expects no more
from Alexander than from Irus.

§ 6

GIVE not only unto feven, but alfo unto
eight, [a] that is unto more than many.
Though to give unto every one that
asketh [b] may feem fevere advice, yet give
thou alfo before asking; that is, where
want is filently clamorous, and mens
neceffities not their tongues do loudly
call for thy mercies. For though fometimes neceffitoufnefs be dumb, or mifery
fpeak not out, yet true charity is
fagacious, and will find out hints for
beneficence. Acquaint thyfelf with the
phyfiognomy of want, and let the dead
colours and firft lines of neceffity fuffice
to tell thee there is an object for thy
bounty. Spare not where thou canft not
eafily be prodigal, and fear not to be
undone by mercy: for fince he who hath

[a] Ecclefiafticus.   [b] Luke.

pity on the poor lendeth unto the Almighty rewarder, who obferves no [a] ides but every day for his payments, charity becomes pious ufury, chriftian liberality the moft thriving induftry; and what we adventure in a cockboat, may return in a carrack unto us. He who thus cafts his bread upon the water, shall furely find it again; for though it falleth to the bottom, it finks but like the ax of the prophet, to rife again unto him.

§ 7

IF avarice be thy vice, yet make it not thy punishment. Miferable men commiferate not themfelves, bowellefs unto others, and mercilefs unto their own bowels. Let the fruition of things blefs the poffeffion of them, and think it more

[a] The ides was the time when money lent out at intereft was commonly repaid.

----Fœnerator Alphius
Suam relegit Idibus pecuniam,
Quærit calendis ponere.   HOR.

satisfaction to live richly than die rich. For since thy good works, not thy goods, will follow thee; since wealth is an appertinance of life, and no dead man is rich; to famish in plenty, and live poorly to die rich, were a multiplying improvement in madness, and use upon use in folly.

§ 8

TRUST not to the omnipotency of gold, and say not unto it thou art my confidence. Kiss not thy hand to that terrestrial sun, nor bore thy ear unto its servitude. A slave unto mammon makes no servant unto GOD. Covetousness cracks the sinews of faith; numbs the apprehension of any thing above sense; and only affected with the certainty of things present, makes a peradventure of things to come; lives but unto one world, nor hopes but fears another; makes their own death sweet unto others, bitter unto themfelves; brings formal fadnefs, fcenical mourning, and no wet eyes at the grave.

§ 9

PERSONS lightly dipt, not ^a grain'd in generous honefty, are but pale in good-nefs, and faint hued in integrity. But be thou what thou virtuoufly art, and let not the ocean wash away thy tincture. Stand ^b magnetically upon that axis, when prudent fimplicity hath fixt there; and let no attraction invert the poles of thy honefty. That vice may be uneafy and even monftrous unto thee, let iterated good acts and long confirmed habits make virtue almoft natural, or a fecond nature in thee. Since virtuous fuperftructions have commonly generous foundations, dive into thy inclinations,

^a Not deeply tinged, not died in grain.

^b That is, "with a pofition as immutable as that of "the magnetical axis," which is popularly fuppofed to be invariably parallel to the meridial, or to ftand exactly north and fouth.

and early difcover what nature bids thee
to be, or tells thee thou may'ft be. They
who thus timely defcend into themfelves,
and cultivate the good feeds which
nature hath fet in them, prove not
shrubs but cedars in their generation.
And to be in the form of ᵃ the beft of the
bad, or the worft of the good, will be no
fatisfaction unto them.

§ 10

MAKE not the confequence of virtue the
ends thereof. Be not beneficent for a
name or cymbal of applaufe; nor exact
and juft in commerce for the advantages
of truft and credit, which attend the reputation of true and punctual dealing:
for thefe rewards, though unfought for,
plain virtue will bring with her. To have
other by-ends in good actions fowers
laudable performances, which muft have

ᵃ Optimi malorum peffimi bonorum. *Firft edit.*

73

deeper roots, motives, and inſtigations, to give them the ſtamp of virtues.

§ 11

LET not the law of thy country be the non ultra of thy honeſty; nor think that always good enough which the law will make good. Narrow not the law of charity, equity, mercy. Join goſpel righteouſneſs with legal right. Be not a mere Gamaliel in the faith, but let the ſermon in the mount be thy [a] Targum unto the law of Sinai.

§ 12

LIVE by old ethicks and the claſſical rules of honeſty. Put no new names or notions upon authentick virtues and vices. Think not, that morality is ambulatory; that vices in one age are not vices in another; or that virtues, which are under the everlaſting ſeal of right reaſon,

[a] A paraphraſe or amplification.

may be ftamped by opinion. And therefore though vicious times invert the
opinions of things, and fet up new ethicks
againft virtue, yet hold thou unto old
morality; and rather than follow a multitude to do evil, ftand like Pompey's pillar
confpicuous by thyself, and fingle in integrity. And fince the worft of times
afford imitable examples of virtue; fince
no deluge of vice is like to be fo general
but more than ª eight will efcape; eye
well thofe heroes who have held their
heads above water, who have touched
pitch and not been defiled, and in the
common contagion have remained un-
corrupted.

§ 13

LET age not envy draw wrinkles on thy
cheeks; be content to be envy'd, but envy
not. Emulation may be plaufible and
indignation allowable, but admit no
treaty with that paffion which no cir-

ª Alluding to the flood of Noah.

cumſtance can make good. A difplacency at the good of others because
they enjoy it, though not unworthy of
it, is an abſurd depravity, ſticking faſt
unto corrupted nature, and often too
hard for humility and charity, the great
ſuppreſſors of envy. This ſurely is a lion
not to be ſtrangled but by Hercules himſelf, or the higheſt ſtreſs of our minds,
and an atom of that power which ſub-
dueth all things unto it ſelf.

§ 14

OWE not thy humility unto humiliation
from adverſity, but look humbly down
in that ſtate when others look upwards
upon thee. Think not thy own shadow
longer than that of others, nor delight
to take the altitude of thyſelf. Be patient
in the age of pride, when men live by
short intervals of reaſon under the dominion of humor and paſſion, when it's
in the power of every one to transform

thee out of thyſelf, and run thee into the ſhort madneſs. If you cannot imitate JOB, yet come not ſhort of [a] SOCRATES, and thoſe patient Pagans who tired the tongues of their enemies, while they perceived they ſpit their malice at brazen walls and ſtatues.

§ 15

LET not the ſun in capricorn [b] go down upon thy wrath, but write thy wrongs in ashes. Draw the curtain of night upon injuries, ſhut them up in the [c] tower of

[a]   ----Dulcique ſenex vicinus Hymetto,
   Qui partem acceptæ ſæva inter vincla cicutæ
   Accuſatori nollet dare.   JUV.
   Not ſo mild Thales, nor Chryſippus thought;
   Nor the good man who drank the pois'nous draught
   With mind ſerene, and cou'd not wiſh to ſee
   His vile accuſer drink as deep as he:
   Exalted Socrates!————   CREECH.

[b] Even when the days are ſhorteſt. *Firſt edit.*

[c] Alluding unto the tower of oblivion mentioned by Procopius, which was the name of a tower of impriſonment among the Perſians: whoever was put therein was as it were buried alive, and it was death for any but to name him. *Firſt edit.*

oblivion, and let them be as though they had not been. To forgive our enemies, yet hope that G OD will punish them, is not to forgive enough. To forgive them ourſelves, and not to pray G OD to forgive them, is a partial piece of charity. Forgive thine enemies totally, and without any reſerve that, however, G OD will revenge thee.

§ 16

WHILE thou ſo hotly diſclaimeſt the devil, be not guilty of diaboliſm. Fall not into one name with that unclean ſpirit, nor act his nature whom thou ſo much abhorreſt; that is, to accuſe, calumniate, backbite, whiſper, detract, or finiſtrously interpret others. Degenerous depravities, and narrow-minded vices! not only below St. PAUL's noble chriſtian but ª ARISTOTLE's true gentleman. Truſt not with ſome that the epiſtle

ª See Ariſtotle's Ethicks, chapter of Magnanimity. *Note to the firſt edit.*

78

of St. JAMES is apocryphal, and fo read with lefs fear that ftabbing truth, that in company with this vice "thy religion is "in vain." MOSES broke the tables, without breaking of the law; but where charity is broke, the law itfelf is shattered, which cannot be whole without LOVE, which is "the fulfilling of it." Look humbly upon thy virtues; and though thou art rich in fome, yet think thyfelf poor and naked without that crowning grace, which "thinketh no evil, which "envieth not, which beareth, hopeth, "believeth, endureth all things." With thefe fure graces, while bufy tongues are cryiug out for a drop of cold water, mutes may be in happinefs, and fing the ᵃ Trifagion in heaven.

§ 17

HOWEVER thy underftanding may waver in the theories of true and falfe,

ᵃ Holy, holy, holy. *Firft edit.*

yet faſten the rudder of thy will, ſteer
ſtraight unto good and fall not foul on
evil. Imagination is apt to rove, and
conjecture to keep no bounds. Some
have run out ſo far, as to fancy the ſtars
might be but the light of the cryſtalline
heaven shot through perforations on the
bodies of the orbs. Others more in-
geniously doubt whether there hath not
been a vaſt tract of land in the Atlantick
ocean, which earthquakes and violent
cauſes have long ago devoured. Specu-
lative miſapprehenſions may be in-
nocuous, but immorality pernicious;
theorical miſtakes and phyſical devia-
tions may condemn our judgments, not
lead us into judgment. But perverſity
of will, immoral and ſinful enormities
walk with [a] Adraſte and Nemeſis at their
backs, purſue us unto judgment, and
leave us viciously miſerable.

[a] The powers of vengeance.

§ 18

BID early defiance unto thofe vices
which are of thine inward family, and
having a root in thy temper plead a right
and propriety in thee. Raife timely
batteries againft thofe ftrong holds built
upon the rock of nature, and make this
a great part of the militia of thy life.
Delude not thyfelf into iniquities from
participation or community, which abate
the fenfe but not the obliquity of them.
To conceive fins lefs, or lefs of fins, becaufe others alfo tranfgrefs, were morally
to commit that natural fallacy of man,
to take comfort from fociety, and think
adverfities lefs becaufe others alfo fuffer
them. The politick nature of vice muft
be oppofed by policy; and, therefore,
wifer honefties projeà and plot againft
it: wherein, notwithftanding, we are not
to reft in generals, or the trite ftratagems
of art. That may fucceed with one,

which may prove fuccefslefs with another: there is no community or commonweal of virtue: every man muſt ſtudy his own œconomy, and adapt ſuch rules unto the figure of himſelf.

§ 19

BE ſubſtantially great in thyſelf, and more than thou appeareſt unto others; and let the world be deceived in thee, as they are in the lights of heaven. Hang early plummets upon the heels of pride, and let ambition have but an ᵃ epicycle and narrow circuit in thee. Meaſure not thyſelf by thy morning shadow, but by the extent of thy grave; and reckon thy-ſelf above the earth, by the line thou muſt be contented with under it. Spread

ᵃ An epicycle is a ſmall revolution made by one planet in the wider orbit of another planet. The meaning is, "Let not ambition form thy circle of "aċtion, but move upon other principles; and let "ambition only operate as ſomething extrinſick and "adventitious."

not into boundlefs expanfions either of defigns or defires. Think not that mankind liveth but for a few; and that the reft are born but to ferve thofe ambitions, which make but flies of men and wildernefles of whole nations. Swell not into vehement actions which imbroil and confound the earth; but be one of thofe violent ones which force [a] the kingdom of heaven. If thou muft needs rule, be [b] ZENO's king, and enjoy that empire which every man gives himfelf. He who is thus his own monarch contentedly fways the fcepter of himfelf, not envying the glory of crowned heads and elohims of the earth. Could the world unite in the practife of that defpifed train of virtues, which the divine ethicks of our SAVIOUR hath fo inculcated upon us, the furious face of things muft difappear;

[a] Matthew XI.

[b] That is, "the king of the Stoics," whofe founder was ZENO, and who held, that the wife man alone had power and royalty.

Eden would be yet to be found, and the angels might look down, not with pity, but joy upon us.

§ 20

THOUGH the quicknefs of thine ear were able to reach the noife of the moon, which fome think it maketh in its rapid revolution; though the number of thy ears should equal Argus his eyes; yet ftop them all with the [a] wife man's wax, and be deaf unto the fuggeftions of tale-bearers, calumniators, pickthank or malevolent delators, who, while quiet men sleep, fowing the tares of difcord and divifion, diftract the tranquillity of charity and all friendly fociety. Thefe are the tongues that fet the world on fire, cankers of reputation, and, like that of *Jonas* his gourd, wither a good name in a night. Evil fpirits may fit ftill, while

[a] Alluding to the ftory of Ulyffes, who ftopped the ears of his companions with wax when they paffed by the Sirens.

84

thefe fpirits walk about and perform the bufinefs of hell. To fpeak more ftrictly, our corrupted hearts are the factories of the devil, which may be at work without his prefence; for when that circumventing fpirit hath drawn malice, envy, and all unrighteoufnefs unto well rooted habits in his difciples, iniquity then goes on upon its own legs; and if the gate of hell were shut up for a time, vice would ftill be fertile and produce the fruits of hell. Thus when GOD forfakes us, Satan alfo leaves us: for fuch offenders he looks upon as fure and fealed up, and his temptations then needlefs unto them.

§ 21

ANNIHILATE not the mercies of GOD by the oblivion of ingratitude: for oblivion is a kind of annihilation; and for things to be as though they had not been, is like unto never being. Make not thy head a grave, but a repofitory of

GOD's mercies. Though thou hadſt the memory of Seneca, or Simonides, and conſcience the punctual memoriſt within us, yet truſt not to thy remembrance in things which need ᵃ phylacteries. Regiſter not only ſtrange, but merciful occurrences. Let ᵇ Ephemerides not Olympiads give thee account of his mercies: let thy diaries ſtand thick with dutiful mementos and aſterisks of acknowledgment. And to be compleat and forget nothing, date not his mercy from thy nativity; look beyond the world, and before the æra of ADAM.

§ 22

PAINT not the ſepulcher of thy ſelf, and ſtrive not to beautify thy corruption.

ᵃ A phylactery is a writing bound upon the forehead, containing ſomething to be kept conſtantly in mind. This was practiſed by the Jewish doctors with regard to the Moſaic law.

ᵇ Particular journals of every day, not abſtracts comprehending ſeveral years under one notation. An Ephemeris is a diary, an Olympiad is the ſpace of four years.

86

Be not an advocate for thy vices, nor call [a] for many hour-glaffes to juftify thy imperfections. Think not that always good which thou thinkeft thou canft always make good, nor that concealed which the fun doth not behold: that which the fun doth not now fee, will be vifible when the fun is out, and the ftars are fallen from heaven. Mean while there is no darknefs unto confcience; which can fee without light, and in the deepeft obfcurity give a clear draught of things, which the cloud of diffimulation hath conceal'd from all eyes. There is a natural ftanding court within us, examining, acquitting, and condemning at the tribunal of ourfelves; wherein iniquities have their natural [b] thetas and

[a] That is, "do not fpeak much or long in juftifica-"tion of thy faults." The antient pleaders talked by a Clepfydra, or meafurer of time.
[b] Θ a theta infcribed upon the judges teffera or ballot was a mark for death or capital condemnation.

no [a] nocent is abfolved by the verdict of himfelf. And therefore although our tranfgreffions shall be tried at the laft bar, the procefs need not be long: for the judge of all knoweth all, and every man will nakedly know himfelf; and when fo few are like to plead not guilty, the affize muft foon have an end.

§ 23

COMPLY with fome humours, bear with others, but ferve none. Civil complacency confifts with decent honefty: Flattery is a juggler, and no kin unto fincerity. But while thou maintaineft the plain path, and fcorneft to flatter others, fall not into felf-adulation, and become not thine own parafite. Be deaf unto thyfelf, and be not betrayed at home. Self-credulity, pride, and levity lead unto felf-idolatry. There is no [b] Damocles like unto felf-

[a] ————Se
Judice nemo nocens abfolvitur.   JUV.
[b] Damocles was a flatterer of Dionyfius.

88

opinion, nor any Siren to our own fawn-
ing conceptions. To magnify our minor
things, or hug ourſelves in our [a] appari-
tions; to afford a credulous ear unto the
[b] clawing ſuggeſtions of fancy; to paſs
our days in painted miſtakes of ourſelves;
and tho' [c] we behold our own blood, to
think ourſelves the [d] ſons of Jupiter; are
blandishments of ſelf-love, worſe than
outward deluſion. By this impoſture
wiſe men ſometimes are miſtaken in their
elevation, and look above themſelves.
And fools, which are [e] antipodes unto
the wiſe, conceive themſelves to be but
their [f] Periœci, and in the ſame parallel
with them.

[a] Appearances without realities.
[b] Tickling, flattering. A clawback is an old word
for a flatterer. Jewel calls ſome writers for popery
"the pope's clawbacks."
[c] That is, "though we bleed when we are wounded,
"though we find in ourſelves the imperfections of
"humanity."
[d] As Alexander the Great did. *Firſt edit.*
[e] Oppoſites.
[f] Only placed at a diſtance in the ſame line.

§ 24

BE not a Hercules furens abroad, and a poltron within thyfelf. To chafe our enemies out of the field, and be led captive by our vices; to beat down our foes, and fall down to our concupifcences; are folecifms in moral fchools, and no laurel attends them. To well manage our affections, and wild horfes of Plato, are the higheft [a] Circenfes: and the nobleft [b] digladiation is in the theatre of ourfelves; for therein our inward antagonifts, not only like common gladiators, with ordinary weapons and downright blows make at us, but alfo, like [c] retiary and laqueary combatants, with nets, frauds, and entanglements fall upon us. Weapons for fuch combats are not

[a] Circenfes were Roman horfe-races.
[b] Fencing-match.
[c] The Retiarius or Laquearius was a prize-fighter, who entangled his opponent in a net, which by fome dexterous management he threw upon him.

to be forged at [a] Lipara: Vulcan's art doth nothing in this internal militia; wherein not the armour of Achilles, but the armature of St. PAUL, gives the glorious day, and triumphs not leading up into capitols, but up into the higheſt heavens. And, therefore, while ſo many think it the only valour to command and maſter others, ſtudy thou the dominion of thyſelf, and quiet thine own commotions. Let right reaſon be thy [b] Lycurgus, and lift up thy hand unto the law of it: move by the intelligences of the ſuperiour faculties, not by the rapt of paſſion, nor merely by that of temper and conſtitution. They who are merely carried on by the wheel of ſuch inclinations, without the hand and guidance of ſovereign reaſon, are but the [c] automatous part of

[a] The Liparæan islands, near Italy, being volcanos, were fabled to contain the forges of the Cyclops.

[b] Thy lawgiver.

[c] Moved not by choice, but by ſome mechanical impulſe.

mankind, rather lived than living, or at leaft underliving themfelves.

§ 25

LET not fortune, which hath no name in fcripture, have any in thy divinity. Let PROVIDENCE, not chance, have the honour of thy acknowledgments, and be thy Oedipus in contingences. Mark well the paths and winding ways thereof; but be not too wife in the conftruction, or fudden in the application. The hand of PROVIDENCE writes often by abbreviatures, hieroglyphicks or short characters, which, like the ᵃ Laconifm on the wall, are not to be made out but by a hint or key from that SPIRIT which indited them. Leave future occurrences to their uncertainties, think that which is prefent thy own; and fince 'tis eafier to foretel an eclipfe, than a foul day, at

ᵃ The short fentence written on the wall of Belshazzar. See Daniel.

fome diftance, look for little regular below. Attend with patience the uncertainty of things, and what lieth yet unexerted in the chaos of futurity. The uncertainty and ignorance of things to come, makes the world new unto us by unexpected emergencies; whereby we pafs not our days in the trite road of affairs affording no novity; for the novelizing fpirit of man lives by variety, and the new faces of things.

§ 26

THOUGH a contented mind enlargeth the dimenfion of little things; and unto fome 'tis wealth enough not to be poor; and others are well content, if they be but rich enough to be honeft, and to give every man his due: yet fall not into that obfolete affectation of bravery, to throw away thy money, and to reject all honours or honourable ftations in this courtly and fplendid world. Old generofity

is fuperannuated, and fuch contempt
of the world out of date. No man is
now like to refufe the favour of great
ones, or be content to fay unto princes,
ª ftand out of my fun. And if any there
be of fuch antiquated refolutions, they
are not like to be tempted out of them
by great ones; and 'tis fair if they efcape
the name of hypocondriacks from the
genius of latter times, unto whom contempt of the world is the moft con-
temptible opinion; and to be able, like
Bias, to carry all they have about them
were to be the eighth wife-man. However, the old ᵇ tetrick philofophers look'd
always with indignation upon fuch a
face of things; and obferving the un-
natural current of riches, power, and
honour in the world, and withal the
imperfection and demerit of perfons often
advanced unto them, were tempted unto

ª This was the anfwer made by Diogenes to Alexander, who asked him what he had to requeft.
ᵇ Sour, morofe.

94

angry opinions, that affairs were ordered
more by ſtars than reaſon, and that
things went on rather by lottery than
election.

§ 27

I F thy veſſel be but ſmall in the ocean of
this world, if meanneſs of poſſeſſions be
thy allotment upon earth, forget not
thoſe virtues which the great diſpoſer of
all bids thee to entertain from thy
quality and condition; that is, ſubmiſſion, humility, content of mind, and
induſtry. Content may dwell in all
ſtations. To be low, but above contempt,
may be high enough to be happy. But
many of low degree may be higher than
computed, and ſome cubits above the
common commenſuration; for in all
ſtates virtue gives qualifications and
allowances, which make out defects.
Rough diamonds are ſometimes miſtaken
for pebbles; and meanneſs may be rich

in accomplishments, which riches in vain defire. If our merits be above our ftations, if our intrinfecal value be greater than what we go for, or our value than our valuation, and if we ftand higher in GOD's, than in the ᵃ Cenfor's book; it may make fome equitable balance in the inequalities of this world, and there may be no fuch vaft chafm or gulph between difparities as common meafures determine. The DIVINE eye looks upon high and low differently from that of man. They who feem to ftand upon ᵇ Olympus, and high mounted unto our eyes, may be but in the valleys, and low ground unto his; for he looks upon thofe as higheft who neareft approach his DIVINITY, and upon thofe as loweft who are fartheft from it.

ᵃ The book in which the Cenfus, or account of every man's eftate was regiftred among the Romans.
ᵇ An high mountain.

§ 28

WHEN thou lookeſt upon the imperfections of others, allow one eye for what
is laudable in them, and the balance
they have from ſome excellency, which
may render them conſiderable. While
we look with fear or hatred upon the
teeth of the viper, we may behold his
eye with love. In venemous natures
ſomething may be amiable: poiſons
afford antipoiſons: nothing is totally, or
altogether uſeleſly bad. Notable virtues
are ſometimes dashed with notorious
vices, and in ſome vicious tempers have
been found illuſtrious acts of virtue;
which makes ſuch obſervable worth in
ſome actions of king Demetrius, An-
tonius, and Ahab, as are not to be found
in the ſame kind in Ariſtides, Numa, or
David. Conſtancy, generoſity, clemency,
and liberality have been highly con-
ſpicuous in ſome perſons not mark'd out

in other concerns for example or imitation. But fince goodnefs is exemplary in all, if others have not our virtues, let us not be wanting in theirs; nor fcorning them for their vices whereof we are free, be condemned by their virtues wherein we are deficient. There is drofs, alloy, and embafement in all human tempers; and he flieth without wings, who thinks to find ophir or pure metal in any. For perfection is not, like light, center'd in any one body; but, like the difperfed feminalities of vegetables at the creation, fcattered through the whole mafs of the earth, no place producing all and almoft all fome. So that 'tis well, if a perfect man can be made out of many men, and, to the perfect eye of GOD, even out of mankind. Time, which perfects fome things, imperfects alfo others. Could we intimately apprehend the ideated man, and as he ftood in the intellect of GOD upon the firft exertion by

creation, we might more narrowly com-
prehend our prefent degeneration, and
how widely we are fallen from the pure
exemplar and idea of our nature: for
after this corruptive elongation from a
primitive and pure creation, we are
almoft loft in degeneration; and ADAM
hath not only fallen from his CREATOR,
but we ourfelves from ADAM, our [a] Tycho
and primary generator.

§ 29

QUARREL not rashly with adverfities
not yet underftood; and overlook not the
mercies often bound up in them: for we
confider not fufficiently the good of evils,
nor fairly compute the mercies of PRO-
VIDENCE in things afflictive at firft hand.
The famous Andreas Doria being invited to a feaft by Aloyfio Fiefchi with
defign to kill him, juft the night before

[a] ‘Ο τεύχων qui facit, ‘Ο τυχὼν qui adeptus eft:
he that makes, or he that poffeffes; as Adam might be
faid to contain within him the race of mankind.

fell mercifully into a fit of the gout and fo efcaped that mifchief. When Cato intended to kill himfelf, from a blow which he gave his fervant, who would not reach his fword unto him, his hand fo fwell'd that he had much ado to effect his defign. Hereby any one but a refolved Stoick might have taken a fair hint of confideration, and that fome merciful genius would have contrived his prefervation. To be fagacious in fuch intercurrences is not fuperftition, but wary and pious difcretion; and to contemn fuch hints were to be deaf unto the fpeaking hand of God, wherein [a] Socrates and Cardan would hardly have been miftaken.

§ 30

BREAK not open the gate of deftruction, and make no hafte or buftle unto ruin.

[a] Socrates, and Cardan, perhaps, in imitation of him, talked of an attendant fpirit or genius, that hinted from time to time how they should act.

Poft not heedlesly on unto the non ultra of folly, or precipice of perdition. Let vicious ways have their [a] tropicks and deflexions, and fwim in the waters of fin but as in the [b] Afphaltick lake, though fmeared and defiled, not to fink to the bottom. If thou haft dipt thy foot in the brink, yet venture not over [c] Rubicon. Run not into extremities from whence there is no regreffion. In the vicious ways of the world it mercifully falleth out that we become not extempore wicked, but it taketh fome time and pains to undo ourfelves. We fall not from virtue, like Vulcan from heaven, in a day. Bad difpofitions require fome time to grow into bad habits; bad habits muft undermine good, and often re-

[a] The tropick is the point where the fun turns back.

[b] The lake of Sodom; the waters of which being very falt, and, therefore, heavy, will fcarcely fuffer an animal to fink.

[c] The river, by croffing which Cæfar declared war againft the fenate.

peated acts make us habitually evil: fo
that by gradual depravations, and while
we are but ftaggeringly evil, we are not
left without parenthefes of confiderations, thoughtful rebukes, and merciful
interventions, to recal us unto ourfelves.
For the wifdom of GOD hath methodiz'd
the courfe of things unto the beft advantage of goodnefs, and thinking confidera-
tors overlook not the tract thereof.

§ 31

SINCE men and women have their
proper virtues and vices; and even twins
of different fexes have not only diftinct
coverings in the womb, but differing
qualities and virtuous habits after; tranf-
place not their proprieties, and confound
not their diftinctions. Let mafculine and
feminine accomplishments shine in their
proper orbs, and adorn their refpective
fubjects. However unite not the vices of

both fexes in one; be not monftrous in iniquity, nor hermaphroditically vitious.

§ 32

IF generous honefty, valour, and plain dealing, be the cognifance of thy family, or characteriftick of thy country, hold faft fuch inclinations fuckt in with thy firft breath, and which lay in the cradle with thee. Fall not into transforming degenerations, which under the old name create a new nation. Be not an alien in thine own nation; bring not a Orontes into Tiber; learn the virtues not the vices of thy foreign neighbours, and make thy imitation by difcretion not contagion. Feel fomething of thyfelf in the noble acts of thy anceftors, and find in thine own genius that of thy pre-deceffors. Reft not under the expired

a In Tiberim defluxit Orontes: "Orontes has "mingled her ftream with the Tiber," fays Juvenal, fpeaking of the confluence of foreigners to Rome.

merits of others, shine by thofe of thy own. Flame not like the central fire which enlightneth no eyes, which no man feeth, and moft men think there's no fuch thing to be feen. Add one ray unto the common luftre; add not only to the number but the note of thy generation; and prove not a cloud but an [a] afterisk in thy region.

§ 33

SINCE thou haft an [b] alarum in thy breaft, which tells thee thou haft a living fpirit in thee above two thoufand times in an hour; dull not away thy days in slothful fupinity and the tedioufnefs of doing nothing. To ftrenuous minds there is an inquietude in overquietnefs, and no laborioufnefs in labour; and to tread

[a] A fmall ftar.
[b] The motion of the heart, which beats about fixty times in a minute; or, perhaps, the motion of refpiration, which is nearer to the number mentioned.

a mile after the slow pace of a fnail, or the heavy meafures of the [a] lazy of Brazilia, were a moft tiring pennance, and worfe than a race of fome furlongs at the [b] Olympicks. The rapid courfes of the heavenly bodies are rather imitable by our thoughts, than our corporeal motions; yet the folemn motions of our lives amount unto a greater meafure than is commonly apprehended. Some few men have furrounded the globe of the earth; yet many in the fet loco-motions and movements of their days have meafured the circuit of it, and twenty thoufand miles have been exceeded by them. Move circumfpectly not [c] meticulously, and rather carefully follicitous than anxiously follicitudinous. Think not there is a lion in the way, nor

[a] An animal called more commonly the Sloth, which is faid to be feveral days in climbing a tree.

[b] The Olympick games, of which the race was one of the chief.

[c] Timidly.

walk with leaden fandals in the paths of goodnefs; but in all virtuous motions let prudence determine thy meafures. Strive not to run like Hercules, a furlong in a breath: feftination may prove precipitation; deliberating delay may be wife cunctation, and slownefs no slothfulnefs.

§ 34

SINCE virtuous actions have their own trumpets, and, without any noife from thyfelf, will have their refound abroad; bufy not thy beft member in the encomium of thyself. Praife is a debt we owe unto the virtues of others, and due unto our own from all, whom malice hath not made mutes, or envy ftruck dumb. Fall not, however, into the common prevaricating way of felf-commendation and boafting, by denoting the imperfections of others. He who difcommendeth others obliquely, commendeth himfelf. He who whifpers their infirmities, proclaims his own exemption from them; and, confequently, fays, I am not as this publican, or ᵃ hic niger, whom I talk of. Open oftentation and loud vain-glory is more tolerable than this obliquity, as but containing fome froth, no ink, as but confifting of a perfonal piece of folly, nor complicated with uncharitablenefs. Superfluously we feek a precarious applaufe abroad: every good man hath his ᵇ plaudite within himfelf; and though his tongue be filent, is not without loud cymbals in his breaft. Confcience will become his panegyrift, and never forget to crown and extol him unto himfelf.

ᵃ Hic niger eft, hunc tu Romane caveto.   HOR. *Firft edit.*

This man is vile; here, Roman, fix your mark;
His foul is black, as his complexion's dark.
                                    FRANCIS.

ᵇ Plaudite was the term by which the antient theatrical performers folicited a clap.

§ 35

BLESS not thyſelf only that thou wert born in [a] Athens; but, among thy multiplied acknowledgments, lift up one hand unto heaven, that thou wert born of honeſt parents; that modeſty, humility, patience, and veracity, lay in the ſame egg, and came into the world with thee. From ſuch foundations thou may'ſt be happy in a virtuous [b] precocity, and make an early and long walk in goodneſs; ſo may'ſt thou more naturally feel the contrariety of vice unto nature, and reſiſt ſome by the antidote of thy temper. As charity covers, ſo modeſty preventeth a multitude of ſins; withholding from noon-day vices and brazen-brow'd iniquities, from ſinning on the houſe-top, and painting our follies with the rays of the ſun. Where this

[a] As Socrates did. Athens a place of learning and civility. *Firſt edit.*

[b] A ripeneſs preceding the uſual time.

virtue reigneth, though vice may show its head, it cannot be in its glory. Where shame of fin fets, look not for virtue to arife; for when modefty taketh wing, ^a Aftræa goes foon after.

§ 36

THE heroical vein of mankind runs much in the foldiery, and courageous part of the world; and in that form we ofteneft find men above men. Hiftory is full of the gallantry of that tribe; and when we read their notable acts, we eafily find what a difference there is between a life in ^b Plutarch and in ^c Laërtius. Where true fortitude dwells, loyalty, bounty, friendship, and fidelity may be found. A man may confide in perfons conftituted for noble ends, who dare do and fuffer, and who have a hand

[a] Aftræa Goddefs of juftice and confequently of all virtue. *Firft edit.*
[b] Who wrote the lives, for the moft part, of warriors.
[c] Who wrote the lives of philofophers.

to burn for their country ᵃ and their friend. Small and creeping things are the product of petty fouls. He is like to be miftaken, who makes choice of a covetous man for a friend, or relieth upon the reed of narrow and poltron friendship. Pitiful things are only to be found in the cottages of fuch breafts; but bright thoughts, clear deeds, conftancy, fidelity, bounty, and generous honefty are the gems of noble minds; wherein, to derogate from none, the true heroick English gentleman hath no peer.

ᵃ Like Mutius Sævola.

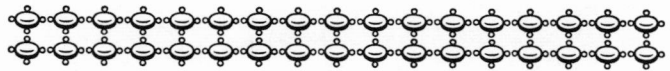

PART II

§ 1

PUNISH not thyfelf with pleafure; glut not thy fenfe with palative delights; nor revenge the contempt of temperance by the penalty of fatiety. Were there an age of delight or any pleafure durable, who would not honour Volupia? but the race of delight is short, and pleafures have mutable faces. The pleafures of one age are not pleafures in another, and their lives fall short of our own. Even in our fenfual days, [a] the ftrength of delight is in its feldomnefs or rarity, and fting in its fatiety: mediocrity is its life, and immoderacy its confufion. The luxurious emperors of old inconfiderately fatiated themfelves with the dainties of fea and land, till,

[a] Voluptates commendat rarior ufus.

wearied through all varieties, their re-
fections became a ftudy unto them, and
they were fain to feed by invention:
novices in true Epicurifm! which by
mediocrity, paucity, quick and healthful appetite, makes delights fmartly
acceptable; whereby Epicurus himfelf
found ^a Jupiter's brain in a piece of
Cytheridian cheefe, and the ^b tongues of
nightingales in a dish of onions. Hereby
healthful and temperate poverty hath
the ftart of naufeating luxury; unto
whofe clear and naked appetite every
meal is a feaft, and in one fingle dish the
firft courfe of ^c Metellus; who are cheaply
hungry, and never lofe their hunger, or
advantage of a craving appetite, becaufe obvious food contents it; while

^a Cerebrum Jovis, for a delicious bit. *Firft edit.*
^b A dish ufed among the luxurious of antiquity.
^c Metellus his riotous pontificial fupper, the great
variety whereat is to be feen in Macrobius. *Firft edit.*
The fupper was not given by Metellus, but by Lentulus when he was made prieft of Mars, and recorded
by Metellus.

ᵃ Nero, half famish'd, could not feed upon a piece of bread, and, lingring after his fnowed water, hardly got down an ordinary cup of ᵇ Calda ᶜ. By fuch circumfcriptions of pleafure the contemned philofophers referved unto themfelves the fecret of delight, which the ᵈ Helluo's of thofe days loft in their exorbitances. In vain we ftudy delight: it is at the command of every fober mind, and in every fenfe born with us: but nature, who teacheth us the rule of pleafure, inftructeth alfo in the bounds thereof, and where its line expireth. And therefore temperate minds, not preffing their pleafures until the fting appeareth, enjoy their contentations contentedly, and without regret, and fo efcape the folly of excefs, to be pleafed unto difplacency.

ᵃ Nero in his flight. Sueton. *Firſt edit.*
ᵇ Warm water.
ᶜ Caldæ gelidæque minifter. *Firſt edit.*
ᵈ Gluttons.

§ 2

BRING candid eyes unto the perufal of mens works, and let not [a] Zoilifm or detraction blaft well-intended labours. He that endureth no faults in men's writings muft only read his own, wherein for the moft part all appeareth white. Quotation miftakes, inadvertency, expedition, and human lapfes, may make not only moles but warts in learned authors; who, notwithftanding being judged by the capital matter, admit not of difparagement. I should unwillingly affirm that CICERO was but slightly verfed in HOMER, becaufe in his work "De Gloria" he afcribed thofe verfes unto Ajax, which were delivered by Hector. What if Plautus in the account of Hercules miftaketh nativity for conception? Who would have mean thoughts of Apollinaris Sidonius, who feems to mif-

[a] From Zoilus the calumniator of HOMER.

take the river Tigris for Euphrates? and
though a good hiftorian and learned
bishop of Avergne had the misfortune
to be out in the ftory of DAVID, making
mention of him when the ark was fent
back by the Philiftins upon a cart; which
was before his time. Though I have no
great opinion of Machiavel's learning,
yet I shall not prefently fay that he was
but a novice in Roman hiftory, becaufe
he was miftaken in placing Commodus
after the emperor Severus. Capital
truths are to be narrowly eyed; collateral
lapfes and circumftantial deliveries not
to be too ftrictly fifted. And if the fubftantial fubject be well forged out, we
need not examine the fparks which
irregularly fly from it.

§3

LET well-weighed confiderations, not
ftiff and peremptory affumptions, guide
thy difcourfes, pen, and actions. To begin

or continue our works like Trifmegiftus of old, "ᵃ verum certè verum atque "veriffimum eft," would found arrogantly unto prefent ears in this ftrict enquiring age; wherein, for the moft part, probably, and perhaps, will hardly ferve to mollify the fpirit of captious contradictors. If Cardan faith that a parrot is a beautiful bird, Scaliger will fet his wits o' work to prove it a deformed animal. The compage of all phyfical truths is not fo clofely jointed, but oppofition may find intrufion; nor always fo clofely maintained, as not to fuffer attrition. Many pofitions feem ᵇ quodlibetically conftituted, and like a ᶜ Delphian blade will cut on both fides. Some truths feem almoft falshoods, and fome falshoods almoft truths; where-

ᵃ In Tabula Smaragdina. *Firft edit.*
"It is true, certainly true, true in the higheft degree."
ᵇ Determinable on either fide.
ᶜ The Delphian fword became proverbial, not becaufe it cut on both fides, but becaufe it was ufed to different purpofes.

in falshood and truth feem almoft æquilibriously ftated, and but a few grains of diftinction to bear down the balance. Some have digged deep, yet glanced by the ᵃ royal vein; and a man may come unto the ᵇ Pericardium, but not the heart of truth. Befides, many things are known, as fome are feen, that is by ᶜ Parallaxis, or at fome diftance from their true and proper beings, the fuperficial regard of things having a different afpect from their true and central natures. And this moves fober pens unto fufpenfory and timorous affer- tions, nor prefently to obtrude them as ᵈ Sibyls leaves, which after confidera- tions may find to be but folious appar- ances, and not the central and vital interiors of truth.

ᵃ I fuppofe the main vein of a mine.

ᵇ The integument of the heart.

ᶜ The parallax of a ftar is the difference between its real and apparent place.

ᵈ On which the Sybil wrote her oraculous anfwers.

VIRGIL.

§ 4

VALUE the judicious, and let not mere acquefts in minor parts of learning gain thy preexiftimation. 'Tis an unjuft way of compute, to magnify a weak head for fome Latin abilities; and to undervalue a folid judgment, becaufe he knows not the genealogy of Hector. When that notable [a] king of France would have his fon to know but one fentence in Latin, had it been a good one, perhaps it had been enough. Natural parts and good judgments rule the world. States are not governed by [b] ergotifms. Many have ruled well, who could not, perhaps, define a commonwealth; and they who underftand not the globe of the earth, command a great part of it. Where natural logick prevails not, artificial too

[a] Lewis the eleventh. Qui nefcit diffimulare nefcit regnare. *Firft edit.*

[b] Conclufions deduced according to the forms of logick.

often faileth. Where nature fills the
fails, the veffel goes fmoothly on; and
when judgment is the pilot, the en-
furance need not be high. When induſtry
builds upon nature, we may expect
pyramids: where that foundation is
wanting, the ſtructure muſt be low. They
do moſt by books, who could do much
without them; and he that chiefly owes
himſelf unto himſelf, is the ſubſtantial
man.

§ 5

LET thy ſtudies be free as thy thoughts
and contemplations: but fly not only
upon the wings of imagination; join
fenſe unto reaſon, and experiment unto
ſpeculation, and ſo give life unto em-
bryon truths, and verities yet in their
chaos. There is nothing more acceptable
unto the ingenious world, than this
noble [a] eluctation of truth; wherein,

[a] Forcible eruption.

againſt the tenacity of prejudice and prefcription, this century now prevaileth. What libraries of new volumes after-times will behold, and in what a new world of knowledge the eyes of our poſterity may be happy, a few ages may joyfully declare; and is but a cold thought unto thoſe, who cannot hope to behold this exantlation of truth, or that obſcured virgin half out of the pit: which might make ſome content with a commutation of the time of their lives, and to commend the fancy of the ᵃ Py-thagorean metempſychoſis; whereby they might hope to enjoy this happineſs in their third or fourth ſelves, and behold that in Pythagoras, which they now but foreſee in ᵇ Euphorbus. The world, which took but ſix days to make, is like to take ſix thouſand to make out: mean

ᵃ Tranſmigration of the ſoul from body to body.
ᵇ Ipſe ego, nam memini, Trojani tempore belli
Panthoides Euphorbus eram.——— OVID.
Note to the firſt edit.

120

while old truths voted down begin to refume their places, and new ones arife upon us; wherein there is no comfort in the happinefs of [a] Tully's Elizium, or any fatisfaction from the ghofts of the antients, who knew fo little of what is now well known. Men difparage not antiquity, who prudently exalt new enquiries; and make not them the judges of truth, who were but fellow enquirers of it. Who can but magnify the endeavours of Ariftotle, and the noble ftart which learning had under him; or lefs than pity the slender progreffion made upon fuch advantages? while many centuries were loft in repetitions and tranfcriptions fealing up the book of knowledge. And therefore rather than to fwell the leaves of learning by fruitlefs repetitions, to fing the fame fong in all ages, nor adventure at effays

[a] Who comforted himfelf that he should there converfe with the old Philofophers. *Firft edit.*

beyond the attempt of others, many would be content that fome would write like [a] Helmont or Paracelfus; and be willing to endure the monftrofity of fome opinions, for divers fingular notions requiting fuch aberrations.

§ 6

DESPISE not the obliquities of younger ways, nor defpair of better things whereof there is yet no profpeƈt. Who would imagine that Diogenes, who in his younger days was a falfifier of money, should in the after-courfe of his life be fo great a contemner of metal? Some Negros who believe the refurreƈtion, think that they shall rife [b] white. Even in this life, regeneration may imitate refurreƈtion; our black and vicious tinƈtures may wear off, and goodnefs

[a] Wild and enthufiaftick authors of romantick chymyftry.
[b] Mandelslo's travels.

clothe us with candour. Good admonitions knock not always in vain. There will be fignal examples of GOD's mercy, and the angels muft not want their charitable rejoices for the converfion of loft finners. Figures of moft angles do neareft approach unto circles, which have no angles at all. Some may be near unto goodnefs, who are conceived far from it; and many things happen, not likely to enfue from any promifes of antecedencies. Culpable beginnings have found commendable conclufions, and infamous courfes pious retractations. Deteftable finners have proved exemplary converts on earth, and may be glorious in the apartment of Mary Magdalen in heaven. Men are not the fame through all divifions of their ages: time, experience, felf-reflexions, and GOD's mercies, make in fome well-temper'd minds a kind of translation before death, and men to differ from themfelves as well as from other perfons. Hereof the old world afforded many examples to the infamy of latter ages, wherein men too often live by the rule of their inclinations; fo that, without any aftral prediction, [a] the firft day gives the laft: men are commonly as they were; or rather, as bad difpofitions run into worfer habits, the evening doth not crown, but fowerly conclude the day.

§ 7

IF the ALMIGHTY will not fpare us according to his merciful capitulation at Sodom; if his goodnefs pleafe not to pafs over a great deal of bad for a fmall pittance of good, or to look upon us in the lump; there is slender hope for mercy, or found prefumption of fulfilling half his will, either in perfons or nations: they who excel in fome virtues being fo often defective in others; few men driving

[a] Primufque dies dedit extremum. *Firft edit.*

at the extent and amplitude of goodnefs, but computing themfelves by their beft parts, and others by their worft, are content to reft in thofe virtues which others commonly want. Which makes this fpeckled face of honefty in the world; and which was the imperfection of the old philofophers and great pretenders unto virtue, who well declining the gaping vices of intemperance, incontinency, violence and oppreffion, were yet blindly peccant in iniquities of clofer faces, were envious, malicious, contemners, fcoffers, cenfurers, and ftuft with vizard vices, no lefs depraving the ethereal particle and diviner portion of man. For envy, malice, hatred, are the qualities of Satan, clofe and dark like himfelf; and where fuch brands fmoke, the foul cannot be white. Vice may be had at all prices; expenfive and coftly iniquities, which make the noife, cannot be every man's fins: but the foul may be fouly ᵃ inquinated at a very low rate; and a man may be cheaply vicious, to the perdition of himſelf.

§ 8

OPINION rides upon the neck of reaſon; and men are happy, wiſe, or learned, according as that empreſs shall ſet them down in the regiſter of reputation. However, weigh not thyſelf in the ſcales of thy own opinion, but let the judgment of the judicious be the ſtandard of thy merit. Self-eſtimation is a flatterer too readily intitling us unto knowledge and abilities, which others ſollicitously labour after, and doubtfully think they attain. Surely, ſuch confident tempers do paſs their days in beſt tranquillity, who, reſting in the opinion of their own abilities, are happily gull'd by ſuch contentation; wherein pride, ſelf-conceit, confidence, and opiniatrity, will hardly

ᵃ Defiled.

fuffer any to complain of imperfection. To think themfelves in the right, or all that right, or only that, which they do or think, is a fallacy of high content; though others laugh in their sleeves, and look upon them as in a deluded ftate of judgment: wherein, notwithftanding, 'twere but a civil piece of complacency to fuffer them to sleep who would not wake, to let them reft in their fecurities, nor by diffent or oppofition to ftagger their contentments.

[a] § 9

SINCE the brow fpeaks often true, fince eyes and nofes have tongues, and the countenance proclaims the heart and inclinations; let obfervation fo far inftruct thee in phyfiognomical lines, as to be fome rule for thy diftinction, and guide for thy affection unto fuch as look moft like men. Mankind, methinks, is

[a] This is a very fanciful and indefenfible fection.

comprehended in a few faces, if we exclude all vifages which any way participate of fymmetries and fchemes of look common unto other animals. For as though man were the extract of the world, in whom all were [a] "in "coagulato," which in their forms were [b] "in foluto" and at extenfion; we often obferve that men do moft act thofe creatures, whofe conftitution, parts, and complexion do moft predominate in their mixtures. This is a corner-ftone in phyfiognomy, and holds fome truth not only in particular perfons but alfo in whole nations. There are, therefore, provincial faces, national lips and nofes, which teftify not only the natures of thofe countries, but of thofe which have them elfewhere. Thus we may make England the whole earth, dividing it not only into Europe, Afia, Africa, but the par-

[a] "In a congealed or compreffed mafs."
[b] "In a ftate of expanfion and feparation."

ticular regions thereof; and may in some latitude affirm, that there are Ægyptians, Scythians, Indians among us, who, though born in England, yet carry the faces and air of those countries, and are also agreeable and correspondent unto their natures. Faces look uniformly unto our eyes: how they appear unto some animals of a more piercing or differing sight, who are able to discover the inequalities, rubbs, and hairiness of the skin, is not without good doubt: and, therefore, in reference unto man, Cupid is said to be blind. Affection should not be too sharp-eyed, and love is not to be made by magnifying glasses. If things were seen as they truly are, the beauty of bodies would be much abridged. And, therefore, the WISE CONTRIVER hath drawn the pictures and outsides of things softly and amiably unto the natural edge of our eyes, not leaving them able to discover those uncomely asperities, which make oyster-shells in good faces, and hedghogs even in Venus's moles.

§ 10

COURT not felicity too far, and weary not the favourable hand of fortune. Glorious actions have their times, extent, and non ultra's. To put no end unto attempts were to make prescription of successes, and to bespeak unhappiness at the last: for the line of our lives is drawn with white and black vicissitudes, wherein the extremes hold seldom one complexion. That Pompey should obtain the sirname of great at twenty-five years, that men in their young and active days should be fortunate and perform notable things, is no observation of deep wonder; they having the strength of their fates before them, nor yet acted their parts in the world for which they were brought into it: whereas men of years, matured for counsels and designs, seem to be beyond the vigour of their active fortunes, and high exploits of life, providentially ordained unto ages beſt agreeable unto them. And, therefore, many brave men finding their fortune grow faint, and feeling its declination, have timely withdrawn themſelves from great attempts, and ſo eſcaped the ends of mighty men, diſproportionable to their beginnings. But magnanimous thoughts have ſo dimmed the eyes of many, that forgetting the very eſſence of fortune, and the viciſſitude of good and evil, they apprehend no bottom in felicity; and ſo have been ſtill tempted on unto mighty actions, reſerved for their deſtructions. For fortune lays the plot of our adverſities in the foundation of our felicities, bleſſing us in the ᵃ firſt quadrate, to blaſt us more sharply in the laſt. And ſince in the higheſt felicities there lieth a capacity

ᵃ That is, "in the firſt part of our time," alluding to the four quadratures of the moon.

of the loweſt miſeries, she hath this
advantage from our happineſs to make
us truly miſerable: for to become acutely
miſerable we are to be firſt happy.
Affliction ſmarts moſt in the moſt happy
ſtate, as having ſomewhat in it of
[a] Belliſarius at beggars bush, or Bajazet
in the grate. And this the fallen angels
ſeverely underſtand; who having acted
their firſt part in heaven, are made
sharply miſerable by tranſition, and
more afflictively feel the contrary ſtate
of hell.

§ 11

CARRY no careleſs eye upon the unexpected ſcenes of things; but ponder
the acts of PROVIDENCE in the publick

[a] Belliſarius, after he had gained many victories, is
ſaid to have been reduced, by the diſpleaſure of the
emperor, to actual beggary: Bajazet, made captive
by Tamerlane, is reported to have been shut up in a
cage. It may ſomewhat gratify thoſe who deſerve to
be gratified, to inform them that both theſe ſtories are
FALSE.

ends of great and notable men, fet out unto the view of all for no common memorandums. The tragical exits and unexpected periods of fome eminent perfons, cannot but amufe confiderate obfervators; wherein, notwithftanding, moft men feem to fee by [a] extramiffion, without reception or felf-reflexion, and conceive themfelves unconcerned by the fallacy of their own exemption: whereas, the mercy of GOD hath fingled out but few to be the fignals of his juftice, leaving the generality of mankind to the pædagogy of example. But the inadvertency of our natures not well apprehending this favourable method and merciful [b] decimation, and that he sheweth in fome what others alfo deferve; they entertain no fenfe of his hand beyond the ftroke of themfelves. Whereupon the whole becomes neceffarily punished, and

[a] By the paffage of fight from the eye to the object.
[b] The felection of every tenth man for punishment, a practice fometimes ufed in general mutinies.

the contracted hand of GOD extended unto univerſal judgments: from whence, neverthelefs, the ſtupidity of our tempers receives but faint impreſſions, and in the moſt tragical ſtate of times holds but ſtarts of good motions. So that to continue us in goodneſs there muſt be iterated returns of miſery, and a circulation in afflictions is neceſſary. And ſince we cannot be wiſe by warnings; ſince plagues are inſignificant, except we be perſonally plagued; ſince alſo we cannot be puniſh'd unto amendment by proxy or commutation, nor by vicinity, but contaction; there is an unhappy neceſſity that we muſt ſmart in our own skins, and the provoked arm of the ALMIGHTY muſt fall upon ourſelves. The capital ſufferings of others are rather our monitions than acquitments. There is but one who died ᵃ ſalvifically for us, and able to ſay unto death, hitherto ſhalt thou go

ᵃ "So as to procure ſalvation."

134

and no farther; only one enlivening death, which makes gardens of graves, and that which was fowed in corruption to arife and flourish in glory: when death itfelf shall die, and living shall have no period; when the damned shall mourn at the funeral of death; when life not death shall be the wages of fin; when the fecond death shall prove a miferable life, and deftruction shall be courted.

§ 12

ALTHOUGH their thoughts may feem too fevere, who think that few ill-natur'd men go to heaven; yet it may be acknowledged that good-natur'd perfons are beft founded for that place; who enter the world with good difpofitions and natural graces, more ready to be advanced by impreffions from above, and chriftianized unto pieties; who carry about them plain and down-right dealing minds, humility, mercy, charity, and

135

virtues acceptable unto GOD and man. But whatever fuccefs they may have as to heaven, they are the acceptable men on earth, and happy is he who hath his quiver full of them for his friends. Thefe are not the dens wherein falshood lurks, and hypocrify hides its head; wherein frowardnefs makes its neft; or where malice, hard-heartednefs, and oppref-fion love to dwell; not thofe by whom the poor get little, and the rich fome times lofe all; men not of retraded looks, but who carry their hearts in their faces, and need not to be look'd upon with per-fpedives; not fordidly or mifchievously ingrateful; who cannot learn to ride upon the neck of the afflicted, nor load the heavy laden, but who keep the [a] temple of Janus shut by peaceable and quiet tempers; who make not only the beft friends, but the beft enemies, as

[a] The temple of Janus among the Romans was shut in time of peace, and opened at a declaration of war.

eafier to forgive than offend, and ready to pafs by the fecond offence before they avenge the firft; who make natural royalifts, obedient fubjects, kind and merciful princes, verified in our own, one of the beft-natur'd kings of this throne. Of the old Roman emperors the beft were the beft-natur'd; though they made but a fmall number, and might be writ in a ring. Many of the reft were as bad men as princes; humourifts rather than of good humours; and of good natural parts rather than of good natures, which did but arm their bad inclinations, and make them wittily wicked.

§ 13

WITH what shift and pains we come into the world, we remember not; but 'tis commonly found no eafy matter to get out of it. Many have ftudied to exafperate the ways of death, but fewer hours have been fpent to foften that neceffity.

That the smoothest way unto the grave is made by bleeding, as common opinion presumeth, beside the sick and fainting languors which accompany that effusion, the experiment in Lucan and [a] Seneca will make us doubt; under which the noble Stoick so deeply laboured, that, to conceal his affliction, he was fain to retire from the sight of his wife, and not ashamed to implore the merciful hand of his physician to shorten his misery therein. [b] Ovid, the old heroes, and the Stoicks, who were so afraid of drowning, as dreading thereby the extinction of their soul, which they conceived to be a fire, stood probably in fear of an easier way of death; wherein the water, entring the possessions of air, makes a temperate suffocation, and kills as it were without

[a] Seneca, having opened his veins, found the blood flow so slowly, and death linger so long, that he was forced to quicken it by going into a warm bath.

[b] Demito naufragium, mors mihi munus erit. *Note to the first edit.*

a fever. Surely many, who have had the
fpirit to deftroy themfelves, have not
been ingenious in the contrivance thereof.
'Twas a dull way practifed by The-
miftocles, [a] to overwhelm himfelf with
bulls-blood, who, being an Athenian,
might have held an eafier theory of death
from the ftate potion of his country; from
which SOCRATES in Plato feemed not to
fuffer much more than from the fit of an
ague. Cato is much to be pitied, who
mangled himfelf with poniards; and
Hannibal feems more fubtle, who carried
his delivery, not in the point but the
[b] pummel of his fword.

[a] Plutarch's lives. *Note to the firft edit.*
[b] Pummel, wherein he is faid to have carried fomething, whereby upon a ftruggle or defpair he might
deliver himfelf from all misfortunes.   *Firft edit.*

JUVENAL fays, it was carried in a ring:

Cannarum vindex, et tanti fanguinis ultor,
Annulus.———

Nor fwords at hand, nor hiffing darts afar,
Are doom'd t' avenge the tedious bloody war,
But poifon drawn thro' a ring's hollow plate.
                              DRYDEN.

139

THE Egyptians were merciful con-
trivers, who deftroyed their malefactors
by afps, charming their fenfes into an
invincible sleep, and killing as it were
with Hermes his [a] rod. The [b] Turkish
emperor, odious for other cruelty, was
herein a remarkable mafter of mercy,
killing his favourite in his sleep, and
fending him from the fhade into the
houfe of darknefs. He who had been thus
deftroyed would hardly have bled at the
prefence of his deftroyer: when men are
already dead by metaphor, and pafs but
from one sleep unto another, wanting
herein the eminent part of feverity, to
feel themfelves to die; and efcaping the
sharpeft attendant of death, the lively
apprehenfion thereof. But to learn to
die, is better than to ftudy the ways of
dying. Death will find fome ways to
untie or cut the moft gordian knots of

[a] Which procured sleep by a touch.
[b] Solyman. Turkish hiftory. *Note to the firft edit.*

140

life, and make mens' miſeries as mortal
as themſelves: whereas evil ſpirits, as
undying ſubſtances, are unſeparable
from their calamities; and, therefore,
they everlaſtingly ſtruggle under their
ᵃ anguſtias, and bound up with immortality can never get out of themſelves.

ᵃ Agonies.

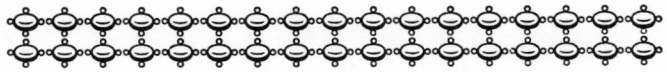

PART III

§ 1

'TIS hard to find a whole age to imitate, or what century to propofe for example. Some have been far more approveable than others; but virtue and vice, panegyricks and fatyrs, fcatteringly to be found in all. Hiftory fets down not only things laudable, but abominable; things which should never have been, or never have been known: fo that noble patterns muft be fetched here and there from fingle perfons, rather than whole nations; and from all nations, rather than any one. The world was early bad, and the firft fin the moft deplorable of any. The younger world afforded the oldeft men, and perhaps the beft and the worft, when length of days made virtuous habits heroical and immoveable, vicious, inveterate, and irreclaimable.

And fince 'tis faid that the imaginations of their hearts were evil, only evil, and continually evil; it may be feared that their fins held pace with their lives; and their longevity fwelling their impieties, the longanimity of GOD would no longer endure fuch vivacious abominations. Their impieties were furely of a deep dye, which required the whole element of water to wash them away, and overwhelmed their memories with themfelves; and fo shut up the firft windows of time, leaving no hiftories of thofe longevous generations, when men might have been properly hiftorians, when ADAM might have read long lectures unto METHUSELAH, and METHUSELAH unto NOAH. For had we been happy in juft hiftorical accounts of that unparallel'd world, we might have been acquainted with wonders; and have underftood not a little of the acts and undertakings of MOSES his mighty men, and men of renown of old; which might have enlarged our thoughts, and made the world older unto us. For the unknown part of time shortens the eſtimation, if not the compute of it. What hath eſcaped our knowledge, falls not under our conſideration; and what is and will be latent, is little better than non-exiſtent.

§ 2

SOME things are dictated for our inſtruction, ſome acted for our imitation; wherein 'tis beſt to aſcend unto the higheſt conformity, and to the honour of the exemplar. He honours GOD, who imitates him; for what we virtuously imitate we approve and admire: and ſince we delight not to imitate inferiors, we aggrandize and magnify thoſe we imitate; ſince alſo we are moſt apt to imitate thoſe we love, we teſtify our affection in our imitation of the inimitable. To affect to be like, may be no imitation: to act, and not to be what we pretend to imitate, is but a mimical conformation, and carrieth no virtue in it. Lucifer imitated not GOD, when he faid he would be like the Higheft; and [a] he imitated not Jupiter, who counterfeited thunder. Where imitation can go no farther, let admiration ftep on, whereof there is no end in the wifeft form of men. Even angels and fpirits have enough to admire in their fublimer natures; admiration being the act of the creature, and not of GOD, who doth not admire himfelf. Created natures allow of fwelling hyperboles: nothing can be faid hyperbolically of GOD, nor will his attributes admit of expreffions above their own [b] exuperances. Trifmegiftus his circle, whofe center is every where, and circumference no where, was no hyperbole. Words cannot exceed, where they cannot exprefs enough. Even the

[a] Salmoneus.   [b] Exaggerations.

moſt winged thoughts fall at the ſetting out, and reach not the portal of DI-VINITY.

§ 3

IN ᵃ bivious theorems, and Janus-faced doctrines, let virtuous conſiderations ſtate the determination. Look upon opinions as thou doſt upon the moon, and chooſe not the dark hemiſphere for thy contemplation. Embrace not the opacous and blind ſide of opinions, but that which looks moſt luciferously or influentially unto goodneſs. 'Tis better to think that there are guardian ſpirits, than that there are no ſpirits to guard us; that vicious perſons are slaves, than that there is any ſervitude in virtue; that times paſt have been better than times preſent, than that times were always bad; and that to be men it ſufficeth to be no better than men in all ages, and

ᵃ Speculations which open different tracks to the mind.

fo promifcuously to fwim down the turbid ftream, and make up the grand confufion. Sow not thy underftanding with opinions, which make nothing of iniquities, and fallaciously extenuate tranfgreffions. Look upon vices and vicious objects, with hyperbolical eyes; and rather enlarge their dimenfions, that their unfeen deformities may not efcape thy fenfe, and their poifonous parts and ftings may appear maffy and monftrous unto thee: for the undif-cerned particles and atoms of evil deceive us, and we are undone by the invifibles of feeming goodnefs. We are only deceived in what is not difcerned, and to err is but to be blind or dim-fighted as to fome perceptions.

§ 4

To be honeft in a [a] right line, and virtu-ous by epitome, be firm unto fuch

[a] Linea recta breviffima. *Firft edit.*

principles of goodnefs, as carry in them volumes of inftruction and may abridge thy labour. And fince inftructions are many, hold clofe unto thofe, whereon the reft depend: fo may we have all in a few, and the law and the prophets in a rule; the Sacred Writ in [a] ftenography, and the Scripture in a nut-shell. To purfue the offeous and folid part of goodnefs, which gives ftability and rectitude to all the reft; to fettle on fundamental virtues, and bid early defiance unto mother-vices, which carry in their bowels the feminals of other iniquities; makes a short cut in goodnefs, and ftrikes not off an head but the whole neck of Hydra. For we are carried into the dark lake, like the Ægyptian river into the fea, by feven principal oftiaries: the [b] mother-fins of that number are the deadly engins of evil fpirits that undo us,

[a] In Short-hand.

[b] Pride, covetoufnefs, luft, envy, gluttony, anger, sloth.

and even evil fpirits themfelves; and he
who is under the chains thereof is not
without a poffeffion. Mary Magdalene
had more than feven devils, if thefe with
their imps were in her; and he who is
thus poffeffed, may literally be named
"Legion." Where fuch plants grow and
profper, look for no champian or region
void of thorns; but productions like the
ᵃ tree of Goa, and forefts of abomination.

§ 5

GUIDE not the hand of GOD, nor order
the finger of the ALMIGHTY unto thy
will and pleafure; but fit quiet in the foft
showers of PROVIDENCE, and favourable diftributions in this world, either to
thyfelf or others. And fince not only
judgments have their errands, but mercies
their commiffions; fnatch not at every

ᵃ Arbor Goa de Ruyz, or Ficus Indica, whofe
branches fend down shoots which root in the ground,
from whence there fucceffively rife others, till one tree
becomes a wood. *Firft edit.*

favour, nor think thyfelf paffed by if they fall upon thy neighbour. Rake not up envious difplacences at things fuccefsful unto others, which the WISE DISPOSER of all thinks not fit for thyfelf. Reconcile the events of things unto both beings, that is, of this world and the next: fo will there not feem fo many riddles in PRO-VIDENCE, nor various inequalities in the difpenfation of things below. If thou doft not anoint thy face, yet put not on fackcloth at the felicities of others. Re-pining at the good, draws on rejoicing at the evils of others: and fo falls into that [a] inhumane vice, for which fo few languages have a name. The bleffed Spirits above rejoice at our happinefs below: but to be glad at the evils of one another, is beyond the malignity of hell; and falls not on evil fpirits, who, tho' they rejoice at our unhappinefs, take no pleafure at the afflictions of their own

[a] Ἐπιχαιρεκακία. *Firft edit.*

fociety or of their fellow natures. Degenerous heads! who muſt be fain to
learn from ſuch examples, and to be
taught from the ſchool of hell.

§ 6

ᵃ GRAIN not thy vicious ſtains; nor
deepen thoſe ſwart tinctures, which
temper, infirmity, or ill habits have ſet
upon thee; and fix not, by iterated depravations, what time might efface, or
virtuous washes expunge. He, who thus
ſtill advanceth in iniquity, deepneth his
deformed hue; turns a shadow into
night, and makes himſelf a Negro in the
black jaundice; and ſo becomes one of
thoſe loſt ones, the diſproportionate pores
of whoſe brains afford no entrance unto
good motions, but reflect and fruſtrate
all counſels, deaf unto the thunder of
the laws, and rocks unto the cries of
charitable commiſerators. He who hath

ᵃ See note (a) page 72.

had the patience of Diogenes, to make orations unto ſtatues, may more ſenſibly apprehend how all words fall to the ground, ſpent upon ſuch a ſurd and ear-leſs generation of men, ſtupid unto all inſtruction, and rather requiring an exorciſt than an orator for their con-verſion!

§ 7

BURDEN not the back of [a] Aries, Leo, or Taurus, with thy faults; nor make Saturn, Mars, or Venus, guilty of thy follies. Think not to faſten thy imper-fections on the ſtars, and ſo deſpairingly conceive thyſelf under a fatality of being evil. Calculate thyſelf within; ſeek not thyſelf in the moon, but in thine own orb or [b] microcoſmical circumference. Let celeſtial aſpects admonish and ad-vertiſe, not conclude and determine thy

[a] The Ram, Lion, or Bull, ſigns in the zodiack.
[b] "In the compaſs of thy own little world."

ways. For since good and bad stars moralize not our actions, and neither excuse or commend, acquit or condemn our good or bad deeds at the present or last bar; since some are astrologically well disposed, who are morally highly vicious; not celestial figures, but virtuous schemes, must denominate and state our actions. If we rightly understood the names whereby GOD calleth the stars; if we knew his name for the dog-star, or by what appellation Jupiter, Mars, and Saturn obey his will; it might be a welcome accession unto astrology, which speaks great things, and is fain to make use of appellations from Greek and barbarick systems. Whatever influences, impulsions, or inclinations there be from the lights above, it were a piece of wisdom to make one of those [a] wise men who overrule their stars, and with their own militia contend with the host of

[a] Sapiens dominabitur astris. *First edit.*

154

heaven. Unto which attempt there want
not auxiliaries from the whole ſtrength
of morality, ſupplies from chriſtian
ethicks, influences alſo and illuminations
from above, more powerful than the
lights of heaven.

§ 8

CONFOUND not the diſtinćtions of thy
life which nature hath divided; that is,
youth, adoleſcence, manhood, and old
age: nor in theſe divided periods, wherein thou art in a manner four, conceive
thyſelf but one. Let every diviſion be
happy in its proper virtues, nor one vice
run through all. Let each diſtinćtion
have its ſalutary tranſition, and critically
deliver thee from the imperfećtions of
the former; ſo ordering the whole, that
prudence and virtue may have the
largeſt sećtion. Do as a child but when
thou art a child, and ride not on a reed
at twenty. He who hath not taken leave

of the follies of his youth, and in his maturer ſtate ſcarce got out of that diviſion, diſproportionately divideth his days, crowds up the latter part of his life, and leaves too narrow a corner for the age of wiſdom; and ſo hath room to be a man, ſcarce longer than he hath been a youth. Rather than to make this confuſion, anticipate the virtues of age, and live long without the infirmities of it. So may'ſt thou count up thy days as ſome do ᵃ ADAM's, that is by anticipation; ſo may'ſt thou be coetaneous unto thy elders, and a father unto thy contemporaries.

§ 9

WHILE others are curious in the choice of good air, and chiefly ſollicitous for healthful habitations, ſtudy thou converſation, and be critical in thy conſortion. The

ᵃ ADAM, thought to be created in the ſtate of man, about thirty years old. *Firſt edit.*

aſpects, conjunctions, and configurations
of the ſtars, which mutually diverſify,
intend, or qualify their influences, are
but the varieties of their nearer or farther
converſation with one another, and like
the conſortion of men, whereby they
become better or worſe, and even ex-
change their natures. Since men live by
examples, and will be imitating ſomething; order thy imitation to thy improvement, not thy ruin. Look not for
roſes in [a] Attalus his garden, or whole-
ſome flowers in a venomous plantation.
And ſince there is ſcarce any one bad,
but ſome others are the worſe for him;
tempt not contagion by proximity, and
hazard not thyſelf in the shadow of corruption. He who hath not early ſuffered
this shipwreck, and in his younger days
eſcaped this Charybdis, may make a
happy voyage, and not come in with

[a] Attalus made a garden which contained only
venomous plants. *Firſt edit.*

157

ᵃ black fails into the port. Self-converfa-tion, or to be alone, is better than fuch confortion. Some fchoolmen tell us, that he is properly alone, with whom in the fame place there is no other of the fame fpecies. Nabuchodonozor was alone, though among the beafts of the field; and a wife man may be tolerably faid to be alone, though with a rabble of people little better than beafts about him. Unthinking heads, who have not learn'd to be alone, are in a prifon to themfelves, if they be not alfo with others: whereas, on the contrary, they whofe thoughts are in a fair, and hurry within, are fome-times fain to retire into company, to be out of the crowd of themfelves. He who muft needs have company, muft needs have fometimes bad company. Be able to be alone. Lofe not the advantage of folitude, and the fociety of thyfelf; nor

ᵃ Alluding to the ftory of Thefeus, who had black fails when he went to engage the Minotaur in Crete.

be only content, but delight to be alone and fingle with OMNIPRESENCY. He who is thus prepared, the day is not uneafy nor the night black unto him. Darknefs may bound his eyes, not his imagination. In his bed he may lie, like [a] Pompey and his fons, in all quarters of the earth; may fpeculate the univerfe, and enjoy the whole world in the hermitage of himfelf. Thus the old Afcetick chriftians found a paradife in a defert, and with little converfe on earth held a converfation in heaven; thus they aftronomiz'd in caves, and though they beheld not the ftars, had the glory of heaven before them.

§ 10

LET the characters of good things ftand indelibly in thy mind, and thy thoughts

[a] Pompeios juvenes Afia atque Europa, fed ipfum Terra tegit Libyes. *Firft edit.*

be active on them. Truft not too much unto fuggeftions from [a] reminifcential amulets, or artificial memorandums. Let the mortifying Janus of [b] Covarrubias be in thy daily thoughts, not only on thy hand and fignets. Rely not alone upon filent and dumb remembrances. Behold not death's heads till thou doeft not fee them, nor look upon mortifying objects till thou overlook'ft them. Forget not how affuefaction unto any thing minorates the paffion from it; how conftant objects lofe their hints, and fteal an

[a] Any thing worn on the hand or body, by way of monition or remembrance.

[b] Don Sebaftian de Covarrubias, writ three centuries of moral emblems in Spanish. In the 88th of the fecond century he fets down two faces averfe, and conjoined Janus-like; the one a gallant beautiful face, the other a death's-head face, with this motto out of Ovid's Metamorphofis,

Quid fuerim, quid fimque, vide.
Firft edit.

—————————You difcern
What now I am, and what I was shall learn.
Addis.

inadvertifement upon us. There is no excufe to forget what every thing prompts unto us. To thoughtful obfervators, the whole world is a ᵃ phylactery; and every thing we fee an item of the wifdom, power, or goodnefs of GOD. Happy are they who verify their amulets, and make their phylacteries fpeak in their lives and actions. To run on in defpight of the re-vulfions and pull-backs of fuch remora's, aggravates our tranfgreffions. When death's-heads on our hands have no influence upon our heads, and fleshlefs cadavers abate not the exorbitances of the flesh; when crucifixes upon mens' hearts fupprefs not their bad commotions, and his image who was murdered for us withholds not from blood and murder; phylacteries prove but formalities, and their defpifed hints sharpen our condemnations.

ᵃ See note (a) page 86.

§ 11

Look not for whales in the Euxine sea,
or expect great matters where they are
not to be found. Seek not for profundity
in shallowneſs, or fertility in a wilderneſs.
Place not the expectation of great happineſs here below, or think to find heaven
on earth; wherein we muſt be content
with embryon-felicities, and fruitions of
doubtful faces: for the circle of our
felicities makes but short arches. In
every clime we are in a ᵃ perifcian ſtate;
and, with our light, our shadow and
darkneſs walk about us. Our contentments ſtand upon the tops of pyramids
ready to fall off, and the inſecurity of
their enjoyments abrupteth our tran-
quillities. What we magnify is magnificent, but, like to the Coloſſus, noble

ᵃ "With shadows all round us." The Perifcii are
thoſe, who, living within the polar circle, ſee the ſun
move round them, and conſequently project their
shadows in all directions.

without, ſtuft with rubbidge and coarſe metal within. Even the ſun, whoſe glorious outſide we behold, may have dark and ſmoky entrails. In vain we admire the luſtre of any thing ſeen: that which is truly glorious, is inviſible. Paradiſe was but a part of the earth, loſt not only to our fruition but our knowledge. And if, according to old dictates, no man can be ſaid to be happy before death; the happineſs of this life goes for nothing before it be over, and while we think ourſelves happy we do but uſurp that name. Certainly, true beatitude groweth not on earth, nor hath this world in it the expectations we have of it. He ſwims in [a] oil, and can hardly avoid ſinking, who hath ſuch light foundations to ſupport him: 'tis, therefore, happy, that we have two worlds to hold on. To enjoy true happineſs, we muſt travel into

[a] Which being a light fluid, cannot ſupport any heavy body.

a very far country, and even out of ourfelves; for the pearl we feek for is not to
be found in the Indian, but in the
ᵃ Empyrean ocean.

§ 12

ANSWER not the fpur of fury, and be
not prodigal or prodigious in revenge.
Make not one in the ᵇ Hiftoria horribilis;
ᶜ flay not thy fervant for a broken glafs,
nor ᵈ pound him in a mortar who
offendeth thee; fupererogate not in the
worft fenfe, and overdo not the neceffities of evil; humour not the injuftice of
revenge. Be not ftoically miftaken in the
equality of fins, nor commutatively

ᵃ "In the expanfes of the higheft heaven."

ᵇ A book fo intitled, wherein are fundry horrid
accounts. *Firft edit.*

ᶜ When Auguftus fupped with one of the Roman
fenators, a slave happened to break a glafs, for which
his mafter ordered him to be thrown into his pond to
feed his lampreys. Auguftus, to punish his cruelty,
ordered all the glaffes in the houfe to be broken.

ᵈ Anaxarchus, an antient philofopher, was beaten
in a mortar by a tyrant.

164

iniquous in the valuation of tranfgreffions; but weigh them in the fcales of
heaven, and by the weights of righteous
reafon. Think that revenge too high,
which is but level with the offence. Let
thy arrows of revenge fly short; or be
aimed like thofe of JONATHAN, to fall
befide the mark. Too many there be to
whom a dead enemy fmells well, and
who find musk and amber in revenge.
The ferity of fuch minds holds no rule
in retaliations, requiring too often a head
for a tooth, and the fupreme revenge for
trefpaffes which a night's reft should
obliterate. But patient meeknefs takes
injuries like pills, not chewing but
fwallowing them down, laconically fuffering, and filently paffing them over; while
angered pride makes a noife, like ᵃ Ho-

ᵃ Tu mifer exclamas, ut Stentora vincere poffis,
Vel potius quantum Gradivus Homericus.   J U V.
Firft edit.
You rage and ftorm, and blafphemously loud,
As Stentor bellowing to the Grecian crowd,
Or Homer's Mars.——   C R E E C H.

165

merican Mars, at every fcratch of offences. Since[a] women do moft delight in revenge, it may feem but feminine manhood to be vindicative. If thou muft needs have thy revenge of thine enemy, with a [b] foft tongue break his bones, heap coals of fire on his head, forgive him and enjoy it. To forgive our enemies is a charming way of revenge, and a short Cæfarian conqueft overcoming without a blow; laying our enemies at our feet, under forrow, shame, and repentance; leaving our foes our friends, and follicitoufly inclined to grateful retaliations. Thus to return upon our adverfaries, is a healing way of re-

[a] ——— Minuti
Semper et infirmi eft animi exiguique voluptas,
Ultio ——— Sic collige, quod vindictâ
Nemo magis gaudet, quam fœmina.   JUV.

——— Revenge! which ftill we find
The weakeft frailty of a feeble mind.
Degenerous paffion, and for man too bafe,
It feats its empire in the female race.   CREECH.

[b] A foft tongue breaketh the bones. PROV. xxv. 15.
Firft edit.

venge; and to do good for evil a foft and melting ultion, a method taught from heaven to keep all fmooth on earth. Common forceable ways make not an end of evil, but leave hatred and malice behind them. An enemy thus reconciled is little to be trufted, as wanting the foundation of love and charity, and but for a time reftrained by difadvantage or inability. If thou haft not mercy for others, yet be not cruel unto thyfelf. To ruminate upon evils, to make critical notes upon injuries, and be too acute in their apprehenfions, is to add unto our own tortures, to feather the arrows of our enemies, to lash ourfelves with the fcorpions of our foes, and to refolve to sleep no more: for injuries long dreamt on, take away at laft all reft; and he sleeps but like Regulus, who bufieth his head about them.

§ 13

AMUSE not thyſelf about the riddles of future things. Study prophecies when they are become hiſtories, and paſt hovering in their cauſes. Eye well things paſt and preſent, and let conjectural ſagacity ſuffice for things to come. There is a ſober latitude for preſcience in contingences of diſcoverable tempers, whereby diſcerning heads ſee ſometimes beyond their eyes, and wiſe men become prophetical. Leave cloudy predictions to their periods, and let appointed ſeaſons have the lot of their accomplishments. 'Tis too early to ſtudy ſuch prophecies before they have been long made, before ſome train of their cauſes have already taken fire, laying open in part what lay obſcure and before buried unto us. For the voice of prophecies is like that of whiſpering-places: they who are near, or at a little diſtance, hear nothing; thoſe at the fartheſt extremity will underſtand all. But a retrograde cognition of times paſt, and things which have already been, is more ſatisfactory than a ſuſpended knowledge of what is yet unexiſtent. And the greateſt part of time being already wrapt up in things behind us; it's now ſomewhat late to bait after things before us; for futurity ſtill ſhortens, and time preſent ſucks in time to come. What is prophetical in one age proves hiſtorical in another, and ſo muſt hold on unto the laſt of time; when there will be no room for prediction, when Janus ſhall loſe one face, and the long beard of time ſhall look like thoſe of DAVID's ſervants, ſhorn away upon one ſide; and when, if the expected ELIAS ſhould appear, he might ſay much of what is paſt, not much of what's to come.

§ 14

LIVE unto the dignity of thy nature, and leave it not difputable at laft, whether thou haft been a man; or, fince thou art a compofition of man and beaft, how thou haft predominantly paffed thy days, to ftate the denomination. Un-man not, therefore, thyfelf by a beftial transformation, nor realize old fables. Expofe not thyfelf by four-footed manners unto monftrous draughts, and caricatura reprefentations. Think not after the old Pythagorean conceit, what beaft thou may'ft be after death. Be not under any brutal [a] metempfychofis while thou liveft, and walkeft about erectly under the fcheme of man. In thine own circumference, as in that of the earth, let the rational horizon be larger than the fenfible, and the circle of reafon than of fenfe: let the divine part be upward, and

[a] See note (a) page 120.

PART THREE

the region of beaſt below; otherwiſe, 'tis
but to live invertedly, and with thy head
unto the heels of thy antipodes. Deſert
not thy title to a divine particle and
union with inviſibles. Let true knowledge and virtue tell the lower world,
thou art a part of the higher. Let thy
thoughts be of things which have not
entred into the hearts of beaſts: think of
things long paſt, and long to come:
acquaint thyſelf with the [a] choragium
of the ſtars, and conſider the vaſt ex-
panſion beyond them. Let intellectual
tubes give thee a glance of things, which
viſive organs reach not. Have a glimpſe
of incomprehenſibles; and thoughts of
things, which thoughts but tenderly
touch. Lodge immaterials in thy head;
aſcend unto inviſibles; fill thy ſpirit with
ſpirituals, with the myſteries of faith, the
magnalities of religion, and thy life with
the honour of GOD; without which,

[a] Dance.

171

though giants in wealth and dignity, we are but dwarfs and pygmies in humanity, and may hold a pitiful rank in that triple divifion of mankind into heroes, men, and beafts. For though human fouls are faid to be equal, yet is there no fmall inequality in their operations; fome maintain the allowable ftation of men; many are far below it; and fome have been fo divine, as to approach the ᵃ Apogeum of their natures, and to be in the confinium of fpirits.

§ 15

BEHOLD thyfelf by inward opticks and the ᵇ cryftalline of thy foul. Strange it is, that in the moft perfect fenfe there should be fo many fallacies, that we are fain to make a doctrine, and often to fee by art. But the greateft imperfection is in our inward fight, that is, to be ghofts

ᵃ To the utmoft point of diftance from earth and earthly things.
ᵇ Alluding to the cryftalline humour of the eye.

unto our own eyes; and while we are fo
sharp-fighted as to look thorough others,
to be invifible unto ourfelves; for the inward eyes are more fallacious than the
outward. The vices we fcoff at in others,
laugh at us within ourfelves. Avarice,
pride, falfhood lie undifcerned and blindly
in us, even to the age of blindnefs: and,
therefore, to fee ourfelves interiourly,
we are fain to borrow other men's eyes;
wherein true friends are good informers,
and cenfurers no bad friends. Confcience
only, that can fee without light, fits in
the ᵃ Areopagy and dark tribunal of our
hearts, furveying our thoughts and condemning their obliquities. Happy is
that ftate of vifion that can fee without
light, though all should look as before
the creation, when there was not an eye
to fee, or light to actuate a vifion:
wherein, notwithftanding, obfcurity is
only imaginable refpectively unto eyes;

ᵃ The great court, like the Areopagus of Athens.

173

for unto G OD there was none: eternal light was ever; created light was for the creation, not himfelf; and as he faw before the fun, may ftill alfo fee without it. In the city of the new Jerufalem there is neither fun nor moon; where glorified eyes muft fee by the ᵃ Archetypal fun, or the light of G OD, able to illuminate intellectual eyes, and make unknown vifions. Intuitive perceptions in fpiritual beings may, perhaps, hold fome analogy unto vifion: but yet how they fee us, or one another, what eye, what light, or what perception is required unto their intuition, is yet dark unto our apprehenfion; and even how they fee G OD, or how unto our glorified eyes the beatifical vifion will be celebrated, another world muft tell us, when perceptions will be new, and we may hope to behold invifibles.

ᵃ Original.

§ 16

WHEN all looks fair about, and thou feeſt not a cloud ſo big as a hand to threaten thee, forget not the wheel of things: think of ſullen viciſſitudes, but beat not thy brains to foreknow them. Be armed againſt ſuch obſcurities, rather by ſubmiſſion than fore-knowledge. The knowledge of future evils mortifies preſent felicities, and there is more content in the uncertainty or ignorance of them. This favour our SAVIOUR vouchſafed unto PETER, when he foretold not his death in plain terms, and ſo by an ambiguous and cloudy delivery dampt not the ſpirit of his diſciples. But in the aſſured fore-knowledge of the deluge, NOAH lived many years under the affliction of a flood; and Jeruſalem was taken unto JEREMY, before it was beſieged. And, therefore, the wiſdom of aſtrologers, who ſpeak of future things, hath wifely foftned the feverity of their doctrines; and even in their fad predictions, while they tell us of inclination not coaction from the ftars, they kill us not with Stygian oaths and mercilefs neceffity, but leave us hopes of evafion.

§ 17

IF thou haft the brow to endure the name of traitor, perjur'd, or oppreffor, yet cover thy face when ingratitude is thrown at thee. If that degenerous vice poffefs thee, hide thyfelf in the shadow of thy shame, and pollute not noble fociety. Grateful ingenuities are content to be obliged within fome compafs of retribution; and being depreffed by the weight of iterated favours, may fo labour under their inabilities of requital, as to abate the content from kindneffes. But narrow felf-ended fouls make prefcription of good offices, and obliged by often favours think others ftill due unto them:

whereas, if they but once fail, they prove
fo perverfely ungrateful, as to make
nothing of former courtefies, and to bury
all that's paft. Such tempers pervert the
generous courfe of things; for they dif-
courage the inclinations of noble minds,
and make beneficency cool unto acts of
obligation, whereby the grateful world
should fubfift, and have their confola-
tion. Common gratitude muft be kept
alive by the additionary fuel of new
courtefies: but generous gratitudes, though
but once well obliged, without quicken-
ing repetitions or expectation of new
favours, have thankful minds for ever;
for they write not their obligations in
fandy but marble memories, which wear
not out but with themfelves.

§ 18

THINK not filence the wifdom of fools;
but, if rightly timed, the honour of wife
men, who have not the infirmity, but

the virtue of taciturnity; and fpeak not out of the abundance, but the well-weighed thoughts of their hearts. Such filence may be eloquence, and fpeak thy worth above the power of words. Make fuch a one thy friend, in whom princes may be happy, and great counfels fuccefsful. Let him have the key of thy heart, who hath the lock of his own, which no temptation can open; where thy fecrets may laftingly lie, like the lamp in Olybius his [a] urn, alive, and light, but clofe and invifible.

§ 19

LET thy oaths be facred, and promifes be made upon the altar of thy heart. Call not Jove [b] to witnefs, with a ftone in one hand, and a ftraw in another; and fo make chaff and ftubble of thy vows.

[a] Which after many hundred years was found burning under ground, and went out as foon as the air came to it. *Firft edit.*

[b] Jovem lapidem jurare. *Firft edit.*

Worldly fpirits, whofe intereft is their belief, make cobwebs of obligations; and, if they can find ways to elude the [a] urn of the Prætor, will truft the thunderbolt of Jupiter: and, therefore, if they should as deeply fwear as [b] Ofman to Bethlem Gabor; yet whether they would be bound by thofe chains, and not find ways to cut fuch Gordian knots, we could have no juft affurance. But honeft mens' words are Stygian oaths, and promifes inviolable. Thefe are not the men for whom the fetters of law were firft forged; they needed not the folemnefs of oaths; [c] by keeping their faith they fwear, and evacuate fuch confirmations.

§ 20

THOUGH the world be hiftrionical, and moft men live ironically, yet be thou

[a] The veffel, into which the ticket of condemnation or acquittal was caft.

[b] See the oath of Sultan Ofman in his life, in the addition to Knolls his Turkish hiftory. *Firft edit.*

[c] Colendo fidem jurant. CURTIUS. *Firft edit.*

what thou fingly art, and perfonate only thyfelf. Swim fmoothly in the ftream of thy nature, and live but one man. To fingle hearts doubling is difcruciating: fuch tempers muft fweat to diffemble, and prove but hypocritical hypocrites. Simulation muft be short: men do not eafily continue a counterfeiting life, or diffemble unto death. He who counterfeiteth, acts a part; and is, as it were, out of himfelf: which, if long, proves fo irkfome, that men are glad to pull off their vizards, and refume themfelves again; no practice being able to naturalize fuch unnaturals, or make a man reft content not to be himfelf. And, therefore, fince fincerity is thy temper, let veracity be thy virtue, in words, manners, and actions. To offer at iniquities, which have fo little foundations in thee, were to be vicious up-hill, and ftrain for thy condemnation. Perfons viciously inclined, want no wheels to make them actively vicious; as having the elater and fpring of their own natures to facilitate their iniquities. And, therefore, fo many, who are finiftrous unto good actions, are ambi-dexterous unto bad; and Vulcans in virtuous paths, Achillefes in vicious motions.

§ 21

REST not in the high-ftrain'd paradoxes of old philofophy, fupported by naked reafon, and the reward of mortal felicity; but labour in the ethicks of faith, built upon heavenly affiftance, and the happinefs of both beings. Underftand the rules, but fwear not unto the doctrines of [a] Zeno or Epicurus. Look beyond [b] Antoninus, and terminate not thy morals in [b] Seneca or [b] Epictetus. Let not the twelve, but the two tables be thy

[a] The authors of the Stoical and Epicurean philofophy.
[b] Stoical philofophers.

law: let Pythagoras be thy remem-
brancer; not thy textuary and final
inſtruĉter; and learn the vanity of the
world, rather from SOLOMON than
ᵃ Phocylides. Sleep not in the dogmas
of the ᵇ Peripatus, Academy, or Porticus.
Be a moraliſt of the ᶜ mount, an Epiĉtetus
in the faith, and chriſtianize thy notions.

§ 22

IN ſeventy or eighty years, a man may
have a deep guſt of the world; know
what it is, what it can afford, and what
'tis to have been a man. Such a latitude
of years may hold a conſiderable corner
in the general map of time; and a man
may have a curt epitome of the whole
courſe thereof in the days of his own life;
may clearly ſee he hath but aĉted over
his fore-fathers; what it was to live in

ᵃ A writer of moral ſentences in verſe.
ᵇ Three ſchools of philoſophy.
ᶜ That is, according to the rules laid down in our
SAVIOUR's ſermon on the mount.

ages paft, and what living will be in all ages to come.

HE is like to be the beft judge of time, who hath lived to fee about the fixtieth part thereof. Perfons of short times may know what 'tis to live, but not the life of man, who, having little behind them, are but Janufes of one face, and know not fingularities enough to raife axioms of this world: but fuch a compafs of years will shew new examples of old things, parallelifms of occurrences through the whole courfe of time, and nothing be monftrous unto him; who may in that time underftand not only the varieties of men, but the variation of himfelf, and how many men he hath been in that extent of time.

HE may have a clofe apprehenfion what it is to be forgotten, while he hath lived to find none who could remember his father, or fcarce the friends of his youth; and may fenfibly fee with what a face in no long time oblivion will look upon himfelf. His progeny may never be his pofterity; he may go out of the world lefs related than he came into it; and, confidering the frequent mortality in friends and relations, in fuch a term of time, he may pafs away divers years in forrow and black habits, and leave none to mourn for himfelf; orbity may be his inheritance, and riches his repentance.

In fuch a thred of time, and long obfervation of men, he may acquire a phyfiognomical intuitive knowledge; judge the interiors by the outfide, and raife conjectures at firft fight; and knowing what men have been, what they are, what children probably will be, may in the prefent age behold a good part and the temper of the next; and fince fo many live by the rules of conftitution, and fo few overcome their temperamental inclinations, make no improbable predictions.

184

Such a portion of time will afford a large profpect backward, and authentick reflections how far he hath performed the great intention of his being, in the honour of his MAKER; whether he hath made good the principles of his nature, and what he was made to be; what characteriftick and fpecial mark he hath left, to be obfervable in his generation; whether he hath lived to purpofe or in vain; and what he hath added, acted, or performed, that might confiderably fpeak him a man.

In fuch an age, delights will be un-delightful, and pleafures grow ftale unto him; antiquated theorems will revive, and ª SOLOMON's maxims be demon-ftrations unto him; hopes or prefumptions be over, and defpair grow up of any fatisfaction below. And having been long toffed in the ocean of this world, he will by that time feel the in-draught

ª That all is vanity.

185

of another, unto which this feems but preparatory, and without it of no high value. He will experimentally find the emptinefs of all things, and the nothing of what is paft; and wifely grounding upon true chriftian expectations, finding fo much paft, will wholly fix upon what is to come. He will long for perpetuity, and live as though he made hafte to be happy. The laft may prove the prime part of his life, and thofe his beft days which he lived neareft heaven.

§ 23

LIVE happy in the Elizium of a virtu-ously compofed mind, and let intellectual contents exceed the delights wherein mere pleafurifts place their paradife. Bear not too slack reins upon pleafure, nor let complexion or contagion betray thee unto the exorbitancy of delight. Make pleafure thy recreation or inter-miffive relaxation, not thy Diana, life and profeffion. Voluptuoufnefs is as infatiable as covetoufnefs. Tranquillity is better than jollity, and to appeafe pain than to invent pleafure. Our hard entrance into the world, our miferable going out of it, our ficknefles, difturbances, and fad rencounters in it, do clamorously tell us we come not into the world to run a race of delight, but to perform the fober acts and ferious purpofes of man; which to omit were foully to mifcarry in the advantage of humanity, to play away an uniterable life, and to have lived in vain. Forget not the capital end, and fruftrate not the opportunity of once living. Dream not of any kind of [a] metempfychofis or tranfanimation, but into thine own body, and that after a long time; and then alfo unto wail or blifs, according to thy firft and fundamental life. Upon a curricle in this world depends a long courfe of

[a] See note (a) page 120.

the next, and upon a narrow fcene here an endlefs expanfion hereafter. In vain fome think to have an end of their beings with their lives. Things cannot get out of their natures, or be or not be in defpight of their conftitutions. Rational exiftences in heaven perish not at all, and but partially on earth: that which is thus once, will in fome way be always: the firft living human foul is ftill alive, and all ADAM hath found no period.

§ 24

SINCE the ftars of heaven do differ in glory; fince it hath pleafed the AL-MIGHTY hand to honour the north-pole with lights above the fouth; fince there are fome ftars fo bright that they can hardly be looked on, fome fo dim that they can fcarce be feen, and vaft numbers not to be feen at all even by artificial eyes; read thou the earth in heaven, and things below from above. Look con-

tentedly upon the scattered difference
of things, and expect not equality, in
luſtre, dignity, or perfection, in regions
or perſons below; where numerous
numbers muſt be content to ſtand like
lacteous or nebulous ſtars, little taken
notice of, or dim in their generations.
All which may be contentedly allowable
in the affairs and ends of this world, and
in ſuſpenſion unto what will be in the
order of things hereafter, and the new
ſyſtem of mankind which will be in the
world to come; when the laſt may be the
firſt, and the firſt the laſt; when Lazarus
may ſit above Cæſar, and the juſt obſcure on earth shall shine like the ſun in
heaven; when perſonations shall ceaſe,
and hiſtrioniſm of happineſs be over;
when reality shall rule, and all shall be
as they shall be for ever.

§ 25

WHEN the Stoick faid that [a] life would not be accepted, if it were offered unto fuch as knew it, he fpoke too meanly of that ftate of being which placeth us in the form of men. It more depreciates the value of this life, that men would not live it over again; for although they would ftill live on, yet few or none can endure to think of being twice the fame men upon earth, and fome had rather never have lived than to tread over their days once more. [b] Cicero in a profperous ftate had not the patience to think of beginning in a cradle again. JOB would not only curfe the day of his nativity, but alfo of his renafcency, if he were to act over his difafters and the miferies of the dunghil. But the greateft under-

[a] Vitam nemo acciperet, fi daretur fcientibus.
SENECA. *Firft edit.*
[b] Si quis Deus mihi largiatur, ut repuerafcam et in cunis vagiam, valde recufem. CIC. de Senectute.

weening of this life is to undervalue that, unto which this is but exordial or a paffage leading unto it. The great advantage of this mean life is thereby to ftand in a capacity of a better; for the colonies of heaven muft be drawn from earth, and the fons of the firft A DAM are only heirs unto the fecond. Thus A DAM came into this world with the power alfo of another; nor only to replenish the earth, but the everlafting manfions of heaven. Where we were when the foundations of the earth were laid, a when the morning ftars fang together, and all the fons of G OD shouted for joy, H E muft anfwer who asked it; who underftands entities of preordination, and beings yet unbeing; who hath in his intellect the ideal exiftences of things, and entities before their extances. Though it looks but like an imaginary kind of exiftency, to be before we are; yet fince

a Job xxxviii.

191

we are under the decree or prefcience of a fure and OMNIPOTENT POWER, it may be fomewhat more than a non-entity, to be in that mind, unto which all things are prefent.

§ 26

IF the end of the world shall have the fame foregoing figns, as the period of empires, ftates, and dominions in it, that is, corruption of manners, inhuman de-generations, and deluge of iniquities; it may be doubted, whether that final time be fo far off, of whofe day and hour there can be no prefcience. But while all men doubt, and none can determine how long the world shall laft, fome may wonder that it hath fpun out fo long and unto our days. For if the ALMIGHTY had not determin'd a fixed duration unto it, according to his mighty and merciful defignments in it; if he had not faid unto it, as he did unto a part of it, hitherto

shalt thou go and no farther; if we confider the inceffant and cutting provocations from the earth; it is not without
amazement, how his patience hath per-
mitted fo long a continuance unto it;
how he, who curfed the earth in the firft
days of the firft man, and drowned it in
the tenth generation after, should thus
laftingly contend with flesh, and yet
defer the laft flames. For fince he is
sharply provoked every moment, yet
punisheth to pardon, and forgives to
forgive again; what patience could be
content to act over fuch viciffitudes, or
accept of repentances which muft have
after-penitences, his goodnefs can only
tell us. And furely if the patience of
HEAVEN were not proportionable unto
the provocations from earth, there needed
an interceffor not only for the fins, but
the duration of this world, and to lead
it up unto the prefent computation.
Without fuch a merciful longanimity, the

heavens would never be fo aged as to grow old like a garment. It were in vain to infer from the doctrine of the fphere, that the time might come, when Capella, a noble northern ftar, would have its motion in the Æquator; that the northern zodiacal figns would at length be the fouthern, the fouthern the northern, and Capricorn become our Cancer. However, therefore, the wifdom of the CREATOR hath ordered the duration of the world, yet fince the end thereof brings the accomplishment of our happinefs, fince fome would be content that it should have no end, fince evil men and fpirits do fear it may be too short, fince good men hope it may not be too long; the prayer of the faints under the altar will be the fupplication of the righteous world, that his mercy would abridge their languishing expectation, and haften the accomplishment of their happy ftate to come.

§ 27

THOUGH good men are often taken away from the evil to come; though fome in evil days have been glad that they were old, nor long to behold the iniquities of a wicked world, or judgments threatened by them; yet is it no fmall fatisfaction unto honeft minds, to leave the world in virtuous well-temper'd times, under a profpect of good to come, and continuation of worthy ways acceptable unto GOD and man. Men who die in deplorable days, which they regretfully behold, have not their eyes clofed with the like content; while they cannot avoid the thoughts of proceeding or growing enormities, difpleafing unto that SPIRIT unto whom they are then going, whofe honour they defire in all times and throughout all generations. If Lucifer could be freed from his difmal place, he would little care though the reft were

left behind. Too many there may be of
^a Nero's mind, who, if their own turn
were ſerved, would not regard what
became of others; and, when they die
themſelves, care not if all perish. But
good men's wishes extend beyond their
lives, for the happineſs of times to come,
and never to be known unto them. And,
therefore, while ſo many queſtion prayers
for the dead, they charitably pray for
thoſe who are not yet alive; they are not
ſo enviously ambitious to go to heaven
by themſelves; they cannot but humbly
wish, that the little flock might be greater,
the narrow gate wider, and that, as many
are called, ſo not a few might be choſen.

§ 28

THAT a greater number of angels remained in heaven, than fell from it, the

^a Nero often had this ſaying in his mouth,

'Εμοῦ θανόντ☉ γαῖα μιχθήτω πυρί:

"when I am once dead, let the earth and fire be
"jumbled together."

196

fchool-men will tell us; that the number of bleſſed fouls will not come short of that vaſt number of fallen ſpirits, we have the favourable calculation of others. What age or century hath fent moſt ſouls unto heaven, he can tell who vouchfaſeth that honour unto them. Though the number of the bleſſed muſt be complete before the world can paſs away; yet ſince the world itſelf ſeems in the wane, and we have no ſuch comfortable prognoſticks of latter times; ſince a greater part of time is ſpun than is to come, and the bleſſed roll already much replenished; happy are thoſe pieties, which ſollicitously look about, and haſten to make one of that already much filled and abbreviated liſt to come.

§ 29

THINK not thy time short in this world, ſince the world itſelf is not long. The created world is but a ſmall parentheſis in eternity; and a short interpofition for a time between fuch a ftate of duration, as was before it and may be after it. And if we should allow of the old tradition, that the world should laft fix thoufand years, it could fcarce have the name of old, fince the firft man lived near a fixth part thereof, and feven Methufelahs would exceed its whole duration. However, to palliate the shortnefs of our lives, and fomewhat to compenfate our brief term in this world, it's good to know as much as we can of it; and alfo, fo far as poffibly in us lieth, to hold fuch a theory of times paft, as though we had feen the fame. He who hath thus confidered the world, as alfo how therein things long paft have been anfwered by things prefent; how matters in one age have been acted over in another; and how there is nothing new under the fun; may conceive himfelf in fome manner to have lived from the

beginning, and to be as old as the world;
and if he should ftill live on, 'twould be
but the fame thing.

§ 30

LASTLY; [a] if length of days be thy
portion, make it not thy expectation.
Reckon not upon long life: think every
day the laft, and live always beyond thy
account. He that fo often furviveth his
expectation lives many lives, and will
fcarce complain of the shortnefs of his
days. Time paft is gone like a shadow;
make time to come prefent. Approxi-
mate thy latter times by prefent apprehenfions of them: be like a neighbour
unto the grave, and think there is but
little to come. And fince there is fome-

[a] Omnem crede diem tibi diluxiffe fupremum,
Grata fuperveniet quæ non fperabitur hora. HOR.

Believe, that ev'ry morning's ray
Hath lighted up thy lateft day;
Then, if to-morrow's fun be thine,
With double luftre shall it shine. FRANCIS.

thing of us that will ftill live on, join both lives together, and live in one but for the other. He who thus ordereth the purpofes of this life, will never be far from the next; and is in fome manner already in it, by a happy conformity, and clofe apprehenfion of it. And if, [a] as we have elfewhere declared, any have been fo happy, as perfonally to underftand chriftian annihilation, extafy, exolution, transformation, the kifs of the fpoufe, and ingreffion into the divine shadow, according to myftical theology, they have already had an handfome antici-pation of heaven; the world is in a manner over, and the earth in ashes unto them.

[a] In his treatife of URNBURIAL. Some other parts of thefe effays are printed in a letter among BROWNE'S pofthumous works. Those references to his own books prove thefe effays to be genuine.

FINIS

NOTES

Greenhill = *Religio Medici, Letter to a Friend, &c. and Christian Morals.* Ed. W. A. Greenhill. 1881.

Keynes = *A Bibliography of Sir Thomas Browne.* By Geoffrey Keynes. 1924.

Wilkin = *Sir Thomas Browne's Works.* Ed. Simon Wilkin. 4 vols. 1835–6.

THE TEXT. This edition has been printed from the edition of 1756. Collation with the first edition (1716) has revealed very few variants of any importance. Differences of spelling have been recorded only when a slight change of sense is involved or when a misprint is corrected. In several instances the punctuation of the first edition has been restored.

Wilkin includes in his notes variant readings from the Sloane MSS. at the British Museum and the Rawlinson MSS. at the Bodleian (Keynes, p. 106); also some passages from the latter portion of *A Letter to a Friend* which were not incorporated in *Christian Morals.* Greenhill also gives the MS. variants and additions in his notes.

p. 3, last line. Browne's mother was Anne, daughter of Paul Garraway, of Lewes.

p. 6, *l.* 6. "It was between 1630 and 1633."

Wilkin, 1, xix.

p. 7. Two unauthorised editions of *Religio Medici* were published in 1642 (Keynes, pp. 4 ff.).

p. 13, *l.* 17. For Latin translations of *Religio Medici* see Keynes 59–67. Merryweather's translation was first published at Leyden in 1644. The editor of the Strasbourg edition (1652) mentioned by Johnson is believed to have been Levin Nicol von Moltke.

The first annotated edition appeared in 1656; the annotator was Thomas Keck (Keynes 6).

p. 14, *l.* 1. John Merryweather was admitted at St John's College, Cambridge, in 1634. He afterwards became a fellow of Magdalene, from which college he took the degree of B.D. in 1652. His book entitled *Directions for the Latine Tongue* was published in 1681.

p. 14, *l.* 14. The full title of Ross' book, published in 1645, is: "*Medicus Medicatus:* or the physicians religion cured, by a lenitive or gentle potion: With some Animadversions upon Sir Kenelme Digbie's Observations on Religio Medici."

p. 15, *l.* 15. "But to pass from these moth-eaten Philosophers, to a *modern* Physician of our own, it was a most unmanly thing in him, while he displays his own *Religion,* to wish that there were a way to propagate the World otherwise than by conjunction with Women...whereby he seems to repine (tho' I understand he was wiv'd a little after) at the honourable degree of *Marriage,* which I hold to be the prime Link of human Society, the chiefest happiness of Mortals, and wherein Heaven hath a special hand."

Howell, *Familiar Letters,* Book I, Sect. 6, Letter LX.

p. 16, *l.* 8. Browne had eleven children (Wilkin).

p. 17, *l.* 4 from bottom. A Dutch translation of *Pseudodoxia Epidemica* appeared in 1668; a German translation in 1680; and French translations in 1733, 1738 and 1753 (Keynes 84–90).

Ross' "Refutation of Doctor Brown's Vulgar Errors" appeared in a work entitled *Arcana Microcosmi* in 1651 (Keynes 218, 219).

p. 19, *l.* 12. *Nature's Cabinet Unlock'd* (Keynes 187). The author is not known.

p. 23, last lines. The parody *Batrachomyomachia* was commonly attributed to Homer. The *Culex* of Virgil describes how a gnat saved the life of a shepherd and was crushed to death in the act; Virgil treats of the bees at the beginning of the fourth *Georgic* (Protinus aerii mellis caelestia dona Exsequar).

Spenser's *Muiopotmos* or *The Fate of the Butterflie* was first published in 1590 and included in *Complaints* in the following year.

Jan van der Wouwer (1574–1612), a pupil of Lipsius and Scaliger, was the author of *Polymathia*, one of the earliest attempts at a survey of the whole field of scholarship.

He produced editions of Petronius, Minucius Felix, and Apollinaris Sidonius and also wrote a small work entitled *Dies Aestiva, sive de Umbra Paegnion* (Hamburg, 1610). In his Prolegomena he quotes the *Batrachomyomachia* and the *Culex*, as well as the σκιαμαχία of Marcus Varro in his own defence.

p. 25, last lines. For *Miscellany Tracts* see Keynes 127–134; and for *Posthumous Works*, 156–162.

p. 26, *l.* 11. Nicolas Claude Fabri de Peiresc (1580–1637) was a famous antiquary, naturalist, and patron of the arts. His life was written in Latin by Gassendus and translated into English by William Rand (1656).

"Après la mort de Peiresc, on trouva plus de dix

mille lettres que lui avaient adressées les savants de France, d'Italie, d'Angleterre, d'Allemagne et des Pays-Bas. La plupart furent détruites par sa nièce et son héritière, qui s'en servait, au rapport de Ménage, pour allumer son feu ou pour se faire des papillotes."

Biographie Universelle (Michaud), XXXII, 377.

p. 29, *l.* 3. J. B. (probably James Boswell, the younger) the annotator of the 1825 edition of Johnson's *Works* (VI, 489) points out that Johnson is wrong here. Howell (*Instructions for Forreine Travell*, p. 39, ed. Arber, 1869) says precisely the opposite: "I have beaten my braines to make one Sentence good *Italian* and congruous *Latin*, but could never do it, but in *Spanish* it is very feasible, as for Example, in this *Stanza,*

> *Infausta Grecia, tu paris Gentes,*
> *Lubricas, sodomiticas, dolosas,*
> *Machinando fraudes cautelosas,*
> *Ruinando animas innocentes*, etc.

which is *Latin* good enough, and yet is it vulgar *Spanish*, intelligible by every plebeian."

J. B. amends Howell's second line to read

> *Lubricas, sed amicitias dolosas.*

p. 31, *l.* 6 from bottom. Berkeley's *Verses on the prospect of planting arts and learning in America* were published in 1752. The last stanza is as follows:

> "Westward the course of empire takes its way;
> The four first Acts already past,
> A fifth shall close the Drama with the day;
> Time's noblest offspring is the last."

p. 32, *l.* 11. The date of the first edition was 1712.

p. 41, *l.* 7. *Hutter's bible.* Elias Hutter (1553–1602), Hebrew professor at Leipzig, produced the Nuremberg Polyglot Bible in 1599. The book contained texts in (1) Hebrew, (2) Chaldee, (3) Greek, (4) Latin, (5) German and (6) Sloven (or Italian or Low German or French).

p. 43, *l.* 4 from bottom. Paolo Sarpi (1552–1623) was the leader of the Venetian Republic in her struggle against the Papacy.

"In her last great encounter with the Curia, she [Venice] was enabled by the genius of one man, Paolo Sarpi, to formulate, and to formulate splendidly, the conception of her political attitude towards Rome. It is the voice of the Servite monk which speaks throughout the struggle...."

H. F. Brown, *Venice*, p. 387.

Johnson wrote a short biography of Paolo Sarpi for *The Gentleman's Magazine* (1738) and issued proposals for a translation of his *History of the Council of Trent*.

p. 44, *l.* 1. Wilkin (I, xlvii) quotes D'Israeli's *Curiosities of Literature* (II, 425) in which Thucydides' character of Themistocles is cited as the best description of the 'stochastic' quality. 'Stochastic' does not occur in Johnson's *Dictionary*.

p. 44, *l.* 6. Cf. Johnson's *Life of Lyttelton*: "He had, in the pride of juvenile confidence, with the help of corrupt conversation, entertained doubts of the truth of Christianity; but he thought the time now come when it was no longer fit to doubt or believe by chance, and applied himself seriously to the great question. His studies, being honest, ended in conviction."

p. 45, *l.* 17. Isaac Watts, *Reliquiae Juveniles* (1734) (Keynes 253).

p. 47, *ll.* 11 ff. In Malone's copy in the Forster Library at South Kensington there is the following note on this passage: "This paragraph, as my friend Archdeacon Kearney observes to me, contains a very happy character of Edmund Burke's style."

Cf. Johnson's description of Burke's eloquence: "Copiousness and fertility of allusion; a power of diversifying his matter, by placing it in various relations....Burke has great knowledge, great fluency of words, and great promptness of ideas, so that he can speak with great illustration on any subject that comes before him."

Boswell, *Tour to the Hebrides* (Hill, v, 215).

p. 63. *The Mythological Picture of Cebes the Theban. Being a serviceable Emblem for the acquiring of Prudence, and the Direction of Human Life.* Translated by Jeremy Collier, 1701.

p. 64, *l.* 9. *hall* ed. 1.

p. 66, *l.* 14. Plutarch, *Alexander*, xxi. As Greenhill observes, it was the daughters, not the sisters, of Darius, who, "as if they had been in a holy temple, or asylum of virgins, rather than in an enemy's camp,...lived unseen and unapproached, in the most sacred privacy."

p. 66, note *a. Metamorphoses*, xii.

p. 66, note *b.* Johnson, not Pope, is wrong. It was Cato Uticensis whose second wife, Marcia, was lent to Quintus Hortensius. (Plutarch, *Cato Minor*, xxv.)

For Pope's reference to this incident see his *Epilogue to Jane Shore.* Pope, however, had Cato

Uticensis in mind when he wrote "To Cato, Virgil paid one honest line" (*Epilogue to the Satires*, II, 120), but afterwards said: "The Aeneid was evidently a party piece: as much as Absalom and Achitophel.—I have formerly said that Virgil wrote one honest line,

'Secretosque pios, his dantem jura Catonem'

and that, I now believe, was not meant of Cato Uticensis." Spence's *Anecdotes*, p. 217.

p. 66, note *c.* τὸ γὰρ "εἰσὶν εὐνοῦχοι οἵτινες εὐνούχισαν ἑαυτοὺς διὰ τὴν βασιλείαν τῶν οὐρανῶν" ἁπλούστερον καὶ νεανικώτερον ἐκλαβὼν ....τὴν σωτήριον φωνὴν ἔργοις ἐπιτελέσαι ὡρμήθη.

Eusebius, *Hist. Eccl.* vi, 8.

For the text too literally interpreted by Origen see S. Matthew xix, 12.

p. 69, *l.* 2. Irus, the beggar of Ithaca, whom Odysseus encountered on his return (*Odyssey*, XVIII).

p. 69, notes. The references are given in the first edition.

p. 70, *l.* 10. 2 Kings vi, 5.

p. 70, *l.* 11. *arise* ed. 1.

p. 70, note *a.* *Epodes*, II, 67.

Johnson omits a line. The accepted text is now:

Haec ubi locutus fenerator Alfius
Iam iam futurus rusticus
Omnem redegit Idibus pecuniam
Quaerit Kalendis ponere.

Redegit for *relegit* was restored by Bentley.

p. 74, *l.* 10. *Targum.* "A paraphrase on the Pentateuch in the Chaldee language."

Johnson's *Dictionary.*

p. 74, *l.* 13. "My dear Sir, never accustom your mind to mingle virtue and vice."

Boswell, *Life* (Hill, II, 427).

p. 75, *l.* 3. *a new Ethicks*, ed. 1.

p. 75, *l.* 6. *Pompey's pillar.* A red granite column standing by itself on the site of the ancient *Serapeum* in Alexandria. It has been conjectured that it was erected by Theodosius to commemorate the victory of Christianity and the destruction of the *Serapeum* (A.D. 391). The pillar was thought in the Middle Ages to mark the site of Pompey's tomb.

p. 77, note *a.* *Satires*, XIII, 185.

p. 77, note *c.* οἱ δὲ κτεῖναι ἄνδρα τοῦ βασιλείου αἵματος οὐδ' ὅλως ἔγνωσαν, ἀλλ' ἐν φρουρίῳ καθεῖρξαι ὅπερ τῆς Λήθης καλεῖν νενομίκασιν.

Procopius, *De Bello Persico*, I, v.

p. 80, *l.* 3 from bottom. Greenhill conjectures that Browne may have written 'Adrastean Nemesis.'

p. 83, *l.* 2 from bottom. *unto us* ed. 1.

p. 83, note *a.* This reference is in the first edition.

p. 84, note *a.*

ἀλλὰ παρὲξ ἐλάαν, ἐπὶ δ' οὔατ' ἀλεῖψαι ἑταίρων
κηρὸν δεψήσας μελιηδέα, μή τις ἀκούσῃ
τῶν ἄλλων. *Odyssey*, XII, 47.

p. 88, note *a.* *Satires*, XIII, 2.

p. 91, *l.* 14. *Rapt.* "A trance; an ecstasy."

Johnson's *Dictionary*.

p. 94, *l.* 13. Bias, who lived in the sixth century B.C., was one of the Seven Wise Men of Greece. When Priene was besieged by Mazares, the inhabitants collected their belongings and prepared to abandon the city. Bias took nothing, declaring "I carry everything with me."

p. 95, *l*. 13. *Sations* ed. 1.

p. 98, *l*. 8. *Temper* ed. 1.

p. 98, *l*. 2 from bottom. *Ideated*. Not in Johnson's *Dictionary*.

p. 99, *l*. 3 from bottom. Andreas Doria (1466–1560), the Genoese admiral who expelled the French and was appointed Perpetual Censor of Genoa.

"Fuit sententia, ut Fliscus Andream... ad coenam, per speciem festivae liberalitatis invitaret.... Interea, Andreae recens, atque improvisa chiragrae tentatio gravem adeo febrem adduxit, ut de salute dubitaretur; quae res, ut Flisco spem ipsius foris opprimendi omnem ademit, sic eundem, ad nova ineunda, atque experiunda consilia prorsus accendit."

Sigonius, *Vita Andreae Doriae*, ii, xxx.

p. 99, note *a*. Johnson's Greek, or at least the printing of it, has been corrected. In the 1756 edition the first line of the note runs: Ὁ τύχων qui facit, Ὁ τυχὼν qui adeptus est.

p. 100, *l*. 2. Plutarch, *Cato Minor*, LXVIII.

p. 100, *l*. 16. "*Jeronimus Cardanus*, that famous Physitian of *Milan*, a great enquirer of truth, but too greedy a receiver of it. He hath left many excellent discourses, Medical, Natural, and Astrological; the most suspitious are those two he wrote by admonition in a dream, that is, *De subtilitate & varietate rerum*." *Vulgar Errors*, i, viii, 13.

p. 103, note *a*. Juvenal, iii, 62.

p. 107, note *a*. *Satires*, i, 4, 85.

p. 109, *l*. 12. "No, Sir; were Socrates and Charles the Twelfth of Sweden both present in any company, and Socrates to say, 'Follow me, and hear a lecture on philosophy'; and Charles, laying his hand on his sword, to say, 'Follow me, and dethrone the Czar'; a man would be ashamed to follow Socrates."

Boswell's *Life* (Hill, III, 265).

Diogenes Laertius (c. 200–250 A.D.) wrote a Greek work on the lives and opinions of the philosophers.

p. 110, note *a.* Mucius Scaevola was ordered to be burnt alive by Porsenna. Thrusting his hand into a fire, Scaevola held it there till it was consumed. Porsenna, astonished at his courage, set him free.

p. 111, note *a.* Juvenal, XI, 208.

p. 112, *l.* 7. The reference, as Greenhill points out, is to Diogenes Laertius, *Epicurus*, VI, 11: Πέμψον μοι τυροῦ, φησί, κυθριδίου, ἵν' ὅταν βούλωμαι πολυτελέσασθαι δύνωμαι. κυθριδίου is Huebner's reading. Variants are κυθριδίον and Κυθηριδίου (Gassendus). Browne's epithet 'Cytheridian' comes from the last of these. Greenhill favours Κυθνίου (Menagius), since the island of Cythnos was famous for its cheeses.

For 'Jupiter's brain' see Athenaeus, *Deipnosophistae*, XII, c. 2, p. 514 and c. 7, p. 529: Διὸς ἅμα καὶ βασιλέως ἐγκέφαλος.

p. 112, note *c.* "Refero enim vobis pontificiis vetustissimam cœnam, quae scripta est in indice quarto Metelli illius pontificis maximi in haec verba: *Ante diem nonum calendas Septembris, quo die Lentulus flamen Martialis inauguratus est, domus ornata fuit....* *Ante cœnam echinos, ostreas crudas quantum vellent, peloridas, sphondilos, turdum, asparagos....*"

Macrobius, *Saturnalia*, II, ix.

NOTES

p. 113, note *a.* "Fameque et iterum siti interpellante panem quidem sordidum oblatum aspernatus est, aquae autem tepidae aliquantum bibit."

Suetonius, *Nero*, 48, 4.

p. 113, note *c.* Juvenal, v, 31.

p. 114, *l.* 2. Zoilus, a grammarian of Amphipolis who lived in the fourth or third century B.C., attacked the fabulous element in Homer and acquired the title of "Homeromastix."

p. 114, *l.* 13. In his speech before his combat with Ajax, Hector promises, in the event of his own victory, to return the body of Ajax to the Achaeans so that they may build him a tomb ἐπὶ πλατεῖ Ἑλλησπόντῳ and that men may say:

ἀνδρὸς μὲν τόδε σῆμα πάλαι κατατεθνηῶτος,

ὅν ποτ᾽ ἀριστεύοντα κατέκτανε φαίδιμος Ἕκτωρ.

Iliad, VII, 89.

Cicero puts this into the mouth of Ajax (Aulus Gellius, xv, 6).

p. 114, *l.* 17. The birth of Hercules is described in *Amphitruo*, Act v.

p. 114, last line. Apollinaris Sidonius (c. A.D. 431–482) was the son-in-law of the Emperor Avitus and was Bishop of the Auvergne for the last twelve years of his life. His works consist of letters and poems.

In his poem *Ad Magnum Felicem Consulem* he writes (ll. 20–22):

Non coctam Babylona personabo,
Quae largum fluvio patens alumno,
Inclusum bibit hinc et inde Tigrim.

and in his *Eucharisticon* (ll. 18–20):

Quique etiam adsumptum pecorosi de grege Iesse
Afflasti regem, plaustro cum fœderis arcam
Imponens hostis....

Babylon was on the banks of the Euphrates; and the Philistines returned the ark of the Lord (1 Sam. vi) long before David was king.

p. 115, *l.* 8. "Again, it was no less pernicious for Caracalla, Commodus, and Maximinus to make Severus their pattern."

Machiavelli, *The Prince*, xix.

Commodus became emperor in A.D. 180; Severus in A.D. 193.

p. 116, *l.* 1. Hermes Trismegistus was the neo-Platonist of the third century A.D. from whom the books known as *Hermetica* take their name.

"Verba Secretorum Hermetis quae scripta erant in tabula Smaragdi, inter manus eius inventa, in obscuro antro, in quo humatum corpus eius repertum est.

Verum sine mendacio, certum et verissimum. Quod est inferius, est sicut quod est superius.... Et sicut omnes res fuerunt ab uno, meditatione unius. Sic omnes res natae fuerunt ab hac una re, adaptatione. Pater eius est Sol, mater eius Luna. Portavit illud ventus in ventre suo. Nutrix eius terra est.... Itaque vocatus sum Hermes Trismegistus, habens tres partes philosophiae totius mundi..."

Chrysogonus Polydorus, *De Alchemia* (1541), p. 363.

p. 116, note *b.* A 'quodlibet' was a question in philosophy or theology proposed for scholastic disputation.

p. 117, *l.* 3 from bottom. *Apparences* ed. 1. Both forms are found up to the end of the seventeenth century.

p. 118, note *a.* Greenhill notes that this proverb is quoted by Jeremy Taylor (*Sermons*, IV, 531, ed. Eden) and that Eden calls it a proverb of the Emperor Sigismund adopted by Louis XI. The original form of the 'proverbium Sigismundi' was slightly different: "Ignarum esse regnandi, qui simulare nesciret" (Aeneas Sylvius, *In libros Antonii Panormitae poetae.* In prooemium, 1, 17).

p. 120, *l.* 9. *Exantlation.* Exhaustion.

Johnson's *Dictionary.*

p. 120, note *b.* The author of the quotation (*Met.* xv, 161) is not given in the first edition, which has *Trojani in tempore.*

p. 122, *l.* 3. Jean Baptiste van Helmont (1577–1644) turned from medicine to mysticism, but, under the influence of Paracelsus, returned to the study of chemistry and natural philosophy. He was one of the earliest investigators of the chemistry of fluids in the human body and was the author of *Ortus Medicinae:*

Theophrastus Bombastus von Hohenheim (1493–1541), commonly called Paracelsus, was trained in the methods of the alchemists and was one of the pioneers of chemical physiology. His *Chirurgia Magna* was published in 1536.

"All the diet he prescribed his patients was this, to eat what, and how often, they thought fitting themselves, and yet he did most strange cures....He was not onely skilled in naturall Magick (the utmost bounds whereof border on the suburbs of hell) but is charged to converse constantly with familiars." Fuller, *Holy State*, II, 3.

p. 122, note *b.* "They [the inhabitants of Capo Verde] believe the dead will rise again, but that they shall be white, and trade there as the *Europeans* do." *Voyages and Travels of J. Albert de Mandelslo into the East Indies*, 1638–1640. Transl. John Davies. Ed. 2 (1669), Book III, p. 213.

p. 124, note *a.* Seneca, *Oed.* 988.

p. 126, last line. Johnson defines *Opinionatrety* (or *Opiniatry*) as "Obstinacy; inflexibility; determination of mind; stubbornness" and adds: "This word, though it has been tried in different forms, is not yet received, nor is it wanted."

p. 132, note *a.* Johnson's opinion is confirmed by Gibbon: "That he was deprived of his eyes, and reduced by envy to beg his bread, 'Give a penny to Belisarius the general!' is a fiction of later times, which has obtained credit, or rather favour, as a strange example of the vicissitudes of fortune" (*Decline and Fall*, XLIII). Lord Mahon's contention, quoted by Wilkin (IV, 88), that the story "may be established on firm historical grounds" is dealt with in Milman's edition (vol. V, p. 247).

"The *iron cage* in which Bajazet was imprisoned by Tamerlane, so long and so often repeated as a moral lesson, is now rejected as a fable by the modern writers, who smile at the vulgar credulity." *Decline and Fall*, LXV.

p. 136, *l.* 11. *times* ed. 1. *time* ed. 2.

p. 138, note *b.* *Tristia*, I, 2, 52.

p. 139, note *a.* *Plutarch* ed. 1.

p. 139, note *b.* Juvenal, x, 165.

p. 140, *l.* 5. "Not long after his return, he [Solyman], thro the perswasions of his Mother, or rather upon suspicion that *Abraham Bassa* still continu'd a Christian, caus'd him to be murther'd whilst he slept on a Couch in the Court, and which he did to him sleeping, to avoid the vow he had often made him, *that he would never do him any harm whilst he liv'd; Sleep,* it seems, being interpreted by his *Mahometan Casuists* for Death."

Knolles, *The Turkish History* (ed. 1701), i, 269.

Johnson borrowed Peter Garrick's copy of Knolles' *Turkish History* in order to write *Irene*. "Knolles," he wrote, "has displayed all the excellencies that narration can admit."

Rambler 122.

p. 144, *l.* 6. Cf. "It had overcome the patience of *Job,* as it did the meekness of *Moses,* and would surely have mastered any, but the longanimity, and lasting sufferance of God." *Vulgar Errors,* i, iii.

p. 146, *l.* 5 from bottom. *Exuperances.* Overbalance; greater proportion (Johnson). Cf. "And therefore hath *Rome* far less variation than *London;* for, on the West side of *Rome,* are seated the great Continents of *France, Spain,* and *Germany,* which take off the exsuperance, and in some way ballance the vigor of the Eastern parts."

Vulgar Errors, ii, ii.

p. 146, note *a.*

Vidi et crudeles dantem Salmonea poenas,
Dum flammas Iovis et sonitus imitatur Olympi.

Aeneid, vi, 585.

p. 147, *l.* 4. *Bivious.* Not in Johnson's *Dictionary.*

p. 148, *l.* 3. *coufusion* ed. 1.

p. 150, *l.* 8. *Champian.* "An expanse of level open country." *O.E.D.*

p. 151, note. ἐπικαιρεκακία edd. 1 and 2.

p. 155, *l.* 2 from bottom. Cf. "Equitare in harundine longa." Horace, *Satires*, II, 3, 248.

p. 157, note *a.* "Hortos fodiebat, gramina seminabat, et noxia innoxiis permiscebat, eaque omnia veneni succo infecta, velut peculiare munus, amicis mittebat." Justinus, *Historiae Philippicae*, XXXVI, 4.

p. 158, note *a.* Plutarch, *Theseus*, XVII.

p. 159, note *a.* Martial, V, 74.

p. 160, *l.* 11. *unto* ed. 1. *anto* ed. 2.

p. 160, *l.* 12. *Minorates.* "A word not yet admitted into the language" (Johnson).

p. 160, note *b. Emblemas Morales de Don Sebastian de Couarrubias,* Madrid, 1610.

The motto is, in fact, printed:

Quid fuerim, quidq́ sim, vide.

p. 162, *l.* 10. Cf. "Since our longest Sun sets at right descensions, and makes but winter arches, and therefore it cannot be long before we lie down in darknesse, and have our light in ashes."

Hydriotaphia.

p. 162, note *a.* "Περίσκιοι dicuntur Qui arcticum circulum eundem habent cum tropico, aut maiorem." (Stephanus.) Cf. Strabo, II, v, 43.

p. 163, *l.* 1. *Rubbidge.* Johnson, in his *Dictionary,* gives the form *Rubbage,* but says that it is not used.

p. 164, note *b.* Probably Henning Gross, *Tragica, seu tristium historiarum de poenis criminalibus et exitu horribili eorum qui . . . ultionem divinam provocarunt, et mirabiliter perpessi sunt* (Isleben, 1597). [Greenhill.]

216

NOTES

p. 164, note *c.* The senator was Vedius Pollio (Seneca, *De Ira*, III, 40 and *De Clementia*, I, 18).

p. 164, note *d.* The tyrant was Nicocreon, king of Cyprus, who put Anaxarchus to death when he was shipwrecked on the island. Anaxarchus had accompanied Alexander to Asia.

p. 165, note *a.* *Satires*, XIII, 112. The first edition has:

Tu tamen exclamas, ut Stentora vincere possis
Vel saltem quantum Gradivus Homericus.

Johnson's version is the right one.

p. 166, note *a.* *Satires*, XIII, 189 ff.
The third line of the quotation should run:

Ultio. Continuo sic collige, quod vindicta.

p. 166, note *b.* The quotation should be:

"A soft tongue breaketh the bone."

p. 167, *l.* 2. *Ultion.* Not in Johnson's *Dictionary.*

p. 167, *l.* 2 from bottom. Regulus, according to the traditional account, suffered excruciating torture when he returned to Carthage.

p. 171, *l.* 15. *Visive organs.* Cf. "For, this doth happen when the axis of the visive cones, diffused from the object, fall not upon the same plane."
Vulgar Errors, III, xx (*Of Snails*).

p. 171, *l.* 2 from bottom. Johnson defines *Magnality* as "A great thing; something above the common use" and adds that the word is "not used." He quotes, however, from *Vulgar Errors*: "Too greedy of magnalities, we make but favourable experiments concerning welcome truths."

217

p. 176, *l.* 2 from bottom. *Often favours.* Cf. "Use a little wine for thy stomach's sake and thine often infirmities" (1 Tim. v, 23).

p. 178, note *a.* "Quis sane mentis Maximum Olibium connumerandum hic esse neget...quandoquidem tam admirabili arte Lucernam concinnaverit, ut perpetuo fulgore lucens mille et quingentos annos plus minus, Plutoni dicata sub terram accensa permanserit. Nam annum circiter millesimum quingentesimum nostrae Salutis iuxta Athesten municipium Patavinum...reperta est urna fictilis, et in ea altera urnula, in qua erat lucerna adhuc ardens...." Bernardinus Scardeonius, *De Antiquitate urbis Patavii*, i, iii.

The story is quoted by Fortunius Licetus (*De Lucernis Antiquorum reconditis*, ii, 12) and the verses supposed to have been inscribed on the urn are included in the *Anthologia Latina* (ed. Burmann, iv, 397). Burmann has a long note on the epigram and identifies Olybius with Maximus Olybrius.

p. 179, note *b.* "Sultan Osman, By the Grace of God unconquerable Turkish Emperor, Swears by the Highest, Almightiest, and Almighty God's Holiness, by his Kingdom, by the substance of the Heavens, the Sun, the Moon and the Stars, by the Earth, and by all under the Earth, by the Brains and Hairy Scalp of my Mother, by my Head, and all the strength of my Soul and Body, by the Holy great Mahomet, and by my Circumsition...."

Knolles, *The Turkish History* (ed. 1701), ii, 58.

p. 182, *l.* 5. *Phocylides* ed. 1. *Phocylydes* ed. 2. Phocylides was born at Miletus about 560 B.C.

NOTES

p. 182, *l.* 6. Plato's school of philosophy, having been first established in the gymnasium of Academus, was known as the Academy; the Peripatetics were the followers of Aristotle; the Stoics were the disciples of Zeno who taught in the Στοὰ (Porticus) ποικίλη at Athens.

p. 191, note *a.* The reference is given in the first edition.

p. 199, note *a.* *Epistles*, 1, 4, 13.

p. 200, note *a.* Wilkin, in his edition of Browne's *Works* (IV, 59–114), points out the passages taken from *A Letter to a Friend.*